DAZZLE

KING GEORGE V CLASS BATTLESHIP

JAMES TAYLOR

DAZZLE

DISGUISE AND DISRUPTION IN WAR AND ART

NAVAL INSTITUTE PRESS
ANNAPOLIS, MARYLAND

CONTENTS

This edition published and distributed in the United States of America and Canada by the Naval Institute Press, 291 Wood Road, Annapolis, Maryland 21402-5043

www.nip.org

First published in Great Britain in 2016 by

The Pool of London Press

A Division of Casemate Publishers

10 Hythe Bridge Street, Oxford OX1 2EW, UK

and

1950 Lawrence Road, Havertown, PA 19083 USA

www.pooloflondon.com

© James Taylor 2016

Edited by Christopher Westhorp

Interior and Jacket Design by Nicola Bailey

Library of Congress Cataloging Number: 2016946514

ISBN 978 1 59114 636 0

Printed in China by Printworks Global

Illustration credits

Page 2: *Unknown artist*, Britain's Sea Power Is Yours! *1945, (detail) poster, printed for H.M. Stationery Office by Thos. Forman and Sons Ltd., Nottingham and issued by the Admiralty. The vessel depicted is a King George V Class Battleship. Imperial War Museum (PST 14019).*

Pages 4-5: *Charles Pears (1873-1958)* A Dazzled Merchantman, *1918, oil on canvas. Imperial War Museum (ART 2878).*

Right: HMS President *in centenary Dazzle. Getty Images.*

DEDICATION

To my sons Josh and Luke Taylor.

ACKNOWLEDGMENTS

Thanks to the late Rodney Wilkinson, MC, son of Norman Wilkinson, for his insights into his father's work during our meetings at the National Maritime Museum, Greenwich, in the late 1980s and early 1990s; to Angelina Palmer and Camilla Wilkinson: daughter-in-law and granddaughter of Norman Wilkinson for their generous assistance in answering questions about the life and work of their celebrated forebear and permission to reproduce key parts of the text from his autobiography, *A Brush with Life* (1969), and a selection of images for this publication. Gratitude to Professor Roy R. Behrens for his expertise and guidance at the outset and the open access provided in Camoupedia, the most important international online tool for research into camouflage. Recognition of the kind assistance of the staff from the following archives, libraries and museums: the Admiralty Library; British Library; Imperial War Museum; University of Glasgow Library and Archives; National Archives, Kew; National Maritime Museum, Greenwich; National Museum of the Royal Navy, Portsmouth; the Royal Society of Arts; the Southampton City Museums; the Victoria and Albert Museum, and especially Mark Pomeroy, Andrew Potter and Annette Wickham of the Royal Academy of Arts. Professor Hugh Murphy and Dr Martin Bellamy, University of Glasgow; also Liv Taylor, Head of Research, Patternity Studio. Thanks to Edward Yardley who kindly assisted with my queries on Frank Henry Mason and who arranged for the photographic portraits of Mason and examples of his maritime work to be published. Paul Liss and Sacha Llewellyn of Liss Llewellyn Fine Art; and Ken Bryant and Dr R. D. A. Smith (Ru Smith) for their guidance and information relating to the work of Jan Gordon and his associates. Ken kindly provided access to Gordon's private diary. To Mike Carroll of the Schoolhouse Gallery for kindly contacting Michelle Weinberg. Also, Dr Melanie Vandenbrouck and Dr Pieter van der Merwe, National Maritime Museum, Greenwich. To James Brazier for kindly looking through the draft. Appreciation to my editor Christopher Westhorp and designer Nicola Bailey. Finally, a hearty thank you to John Lee of the Pool of London Press for devising the project and offering it to me.

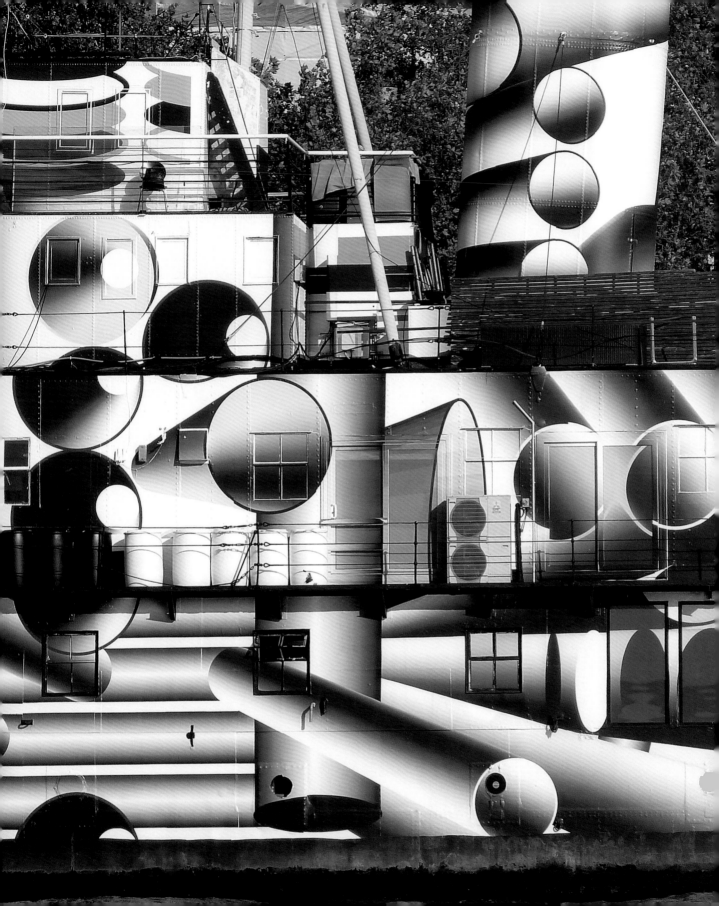

INTRODUCTION

During the First World War thousands of merchant ships and hundreds of naval vessels across the world were coated with Dazzle-painted designs. They were predominately painted in Europe, the United States of America and Canada with vivid, violently contrasting patterns of colour designed to confuse and deceive German U-boat commanders.

The intention of Dazzle painting, also referred to as Dazzle camouflage, was to break up the outline of a ship so that when viewed in haste through an enemy periscope it would make it difficult to estimate the type, speed, range and course of the vessel. As a decision had to be made quickly and the technology was limited, a torpedo was fired in anticipation of where a ship was sailing. It was hoped that Dazzle painting would achieve one of three possible outcomes: to force the attacker to abandon the strike; to misdirect the torpedo away from the vessel; or to misdirect it to a less vulnerable part of the ship, thereby enabling it to escape or possibly fight back.

Dazzle-painted ships constituted the world's largest public art and design display ever assembled. The vast floating 'canvases' prompted one US reporter to note that their fleet looked like 'a flock of sea-going Easter Eggs'. However, the concept of Dazzle painting and its implementation was not credited to a US inventor but instead to the British marine painter Norman Wilkinson. In April 1917, when he came up with the idea and wrote to the British Admiralty outlining his plan, he was serving in a minesweeper off the southwest coast of England.

After the British Admiralty formally approved the scheme, Wilkinson was appointed its operations manager and creative director. The Dazzle Section was established at Burlington House in London, ordinarily

Leonard Campbell Taylor (1874–1969), HM Transport Mauretania entering Sandon Half-Tide Dock, Liverpool, *1919, watercolour. Imperial War Museum (ART 2291).*

magazines, newspapers and published accounts in the archives and libraries of the Admiralty, British Library, Imperial War Museum, National Archives at Kew, National Maritime Museum at Greenwich, Royal Society of Arts and University of Glasgow – offers some fresh perspectives into the origins, principles, development and implementation of Dazzle painting, and the competing camouflage schemes, including the claims and counter-claims between Kerr and Wilkinson. These claims turned into a protracted battle in private and public that, in tandem with Kerr's quest for credit and official recognition, became increasingly bitter.

Kerr acknowledged the significant influence on his work of the American painter and naturalist Abbott Handerson Thayer, who from 1898 had worked with fellow artist George de Forest Brush on ways to utilize natural camouflage principles for military purposes – in particular the so-called countershading that was

the home of the Royal Academy of Arts (RA), also known as the Royal Academy, where designs were tested on ship models before being approved and distributed to supervisors in key British ports to implement them on selected ships.

Early in 1918 Wilkinson was invited to travel to Washington, D.C., to advise the United States Navy Department on Dazzle painting, and he noted in his autobiography that around '1,100 American merchantmen were painted to the designs originated in the London department'.

After the war it was suggested to Wilkinson that he was eligible to apply to the Royal Commission on Awards to Inventors (RCAI) 'for whatever they thought [his] idea merited'. Finally, in October 1922 official confirmation was conferred on the artist when he beat off several rival claimants under cross-examination by legal counsel and was awarded the sum of £2,000 minus legal costs. This remains a significant sum of money today, although it is modest in comparison to the £10,000 – a small fortune then – claimed by his main rival, John Graham Kerr, the Regius Professor of Zoology at the University of Glasgow. In 2016 values, £10,000 in 1922 had risen to a real price value of £441,000, or the economic power value of more than 4 million pounds.

An examination of original documents – including letters, papers and photographs, as well as journals,

patented in the USA as a means to reduce the visibility of ships. Wilkinson tried to avoid using the word camouflage when explaining his scheme, although he did use it on occasions. He was aware that most people mistakenly considered camouflage to mean mainly one thing – invisibility; and for his scheme to be effective it relied on the Dazzled vessel to be visible.

Kerr believed that prior to Wilkinson he had introduced, in the early stages of the war, an identical scheme to the Admiralty. At an Admiralty inquiry that took place in October and November 1920 into the rival claims for Dazzle painting, Kerr wrote: 'I would beg to emphasise that the main question at issue is the truth or untruth of my assertion that "Dazzle" as used during the latter months of the War is simply my scheme of "parti-colouring" with violently contrasting pigments. It will not satisfy me if the Admiralty confine itself to a statement that the "two schemes have points in common".' To this end 40 questions were raised in the British Houses of Parliament. To a lesser extent Kerr's battle for recognition continued even after his death in 1957, when his former pupil Hugh Bamford Cott, who became an eminent zoologist at the University of Cambridge and specialist adviser on camouflage to the British government, took up the challenge.

Beyond this extraordinary hostile debate between artist and scientist, this book addresses the life, work and achievements of Norman Wilkinson: the man behind the Dazzle, and how it was organized and implemented across Britain; it considers if modern art movements prior to and during the war inspired Dazzle, and whether Wilkinson's scheme impacted on any avant-garde artists; it examines the adoption and implementation of Dazzle in the USA; also, its evolution into what became generally known as disruptive camouflage. In the inter-war and post-war periods it shows how the scheme influenced art, architecture, dance, design, fashion, music hall and theatrical performances and even the exterior appearance of motor racing cars; and it features a visual tribute to the vessels that have been painted with brilliant bold patterns inspired by Dazzle to coincide with the First World War commemorations. It concludes with an assessment of whether Dazzle painting actually worked and highlights the commodification of Dazzle through the sale of a wide range of gifts and merchandise, including wallets and wrapping paper.

NORMAN WILKINSON
THE MAN BEHIND THE DAZZLE

Cambridge-born Norman Wilkinson (1878–1971) was an established, versatile and highly regarded marine painter, illustrator, printmaker and poster artist prior to the outbreak of the First World War. His remarkable artistic talent was combined in equal measures with ambition and determination, the perfect combination for a self-employed artist born without the proverbial 'silver spoon'. Angelina Palmer, Wilkinson's daughter-in-law, vividly recalls a charming gentleman of 'around 5 feet 10 inches in height with brilliant blue eyes' who was full of fun and 'capable of making the tears run down your cheeks'.

On July 2015 the British TV programme the 'Ingenious Isles', part of the popular *Coast* series, included a feature on the origins and impact of Dazzle painting led by Dick Strawbridge, a former military man, now active as an engineer-inventor and sustainability expert, who is famous for a walrus moustache that is reminiscent of Bruce Bairnsfather's celebrated First World War comic creation 'Old Bill'. He asked Sarah Phillips, a granddaughter of Norman Wilkinson, about the personal qualities of her forebear. She recalled that he was 'very amusing, very charismatic and very determined'. Strawbridge added it was '...that determination that made him successful where other people weren't'.

By the standards of today Wilkinson was from a large family. His father, Thomas Collins Wilkinson, was a music teacher. He recalled in his autobiography, *A Brush with Life* (1969), that his 'childhood was of no particular interest and I remember little of it', except that my 'mother [Emma] was left, while still young, to bring up four small children'. Not surprisingly, money was in short supply at home.

After a period as a chorister at St. Paul's Cathedral Choir School in London, Wilkinson secured a subsidized

Norman Wilkinson, HMS Campbeltown *at St Nazaire, 27 March 1942, oil on canvas. National Maritime Museum, Greenwich, London.*
[see pages 20–21]

place at Berkhamsted School in Hertfordshire. However, his formal education was over at the age of 16 and he later confessed that his 'standard of education was lamentable' and that his 'lessons were merely an interruption in my wish to draw'.

Wilkinson went to live with his mother, who had moved to Southsea on the south coast of England, close to Portsmouth, and it was here that his passion for maritime art was ignited. In his autobiography he recalled that 'Portsmouth Harbour and Spithead, alive with shipping, were ideal for a youth whose whole interest was ships and the sea'. Initially reluctant, he eventually persuaded his mother to approve his enrolment at the Portsmouth and Southsea School of Art, although a compromise was reached where it was insisted that he should study for an Art Master's certificate, which would enable him to earn some money from teaching.

Palmer recollects that her father-in-law's uncle 'Dick' [Richard Ellis] Wilkinson 'a little known and underappreciated artist' was a formative influence. There is one painting by Dick Wilkinson, entitled *The Jolly Strollers* (1888), in the Russell-Cotes Museum, Bournemouth. In the late 1880s they travelled together to the emerging art colony of St. Ives in Cornwall. Surviving family photographs depict Wilkinson among various artists, including the landscape painters Alfred East (1844–1913) and Adrian Stokes (1854–1935) who became the first president of the St. Ives Society of Artists in 1890. This experience encouraged Wilkinson to return to St. Ives in the 1890s to train with Melbourne-born and Canadian-trained artist Louis Grier (1864–1920).

Wilkinson maintained contact with several artists he met there throughout his life. Initially, Grier with the maritime artist Julius Olsson (1864–1942) ran an art school of landscape and marine painting (established in 1888), before venturing out on his own with the assistance of Algernon Talmage (1871–1939). According to the *Cornish Review* (1950), Talmage was 'modest and slightly reserved' although 'one of the most talented and certainly the most popular of the St. Ives' painters'. His encouragement of working outdoors and demonstrations of loosely executed oil impressions were very popular were students.

Grier and Olsson were partygoers with gregarious personalities. Their art and tuition, alongside Talmage, had a formative influence on Wilkinson. Of a Swedish father and English mother, Olsson was largely self-taught. He was described, by the artist and journalist Alan Gardner Folliott Stokes, in *The Studio* magazine in 1910 (vol.48) as 'A big man with a big heart, who paints big pictures with big brushes'. Like Wilkinson he was an enthusiastic yachtsman and also served as a volunteer in the Royal Navy during the war. His dramatic skies with incandescent clouds, powerful seas, vigorous breaking waves, brilliant lighting effects and preference for high-viewpoints can be detected in many of Wilkinson's works. Wilkinson kept in contact with Olsson, who later assisted him with the Dazzle painting scheme.

Grier shared with Talmage a passion for the work of James Abbott McNeill Whistler (1834–1903) and the French Impressionists. The soft-toned backgrounds of greys and blues favoured by Whistler, animated with details and highlights in vivid touches of colour, can also be found in Wilkinson's canvases. Wilkinson's final period of formal training lasted around six months when he and two artist friends from Cornwall left for Paris in December 1899 to study figure painting and drawing. One of them, Reginald Guy Kortright (1876–1948), also shared Wilkinson's determination to raise the standard of British poster design. He would also assist him with the Dazzle painting scheme, headquartered at Burlington House.

Angelina Palmer cannot recall that Wilkinson ever specified his favourite artists, however she does remember that in his personal collection was a ship drawing by either Willem van de Velde the Elder (*c*.1611–1693), or his son the Younger (1633–1707). The current whereabouts of this drawing has not been determined. In the early 1670s the van de Veldes left Holland to settle in Greenwich, at the invitation of King Charles II, where they used studio space on the south-side ground floor of Inigo Jones' Queen's House (this would become part of the National Maritime Museum after its official opening in 1937) to draw and paint marines for the royal family and the British Admiralty. They worked as a brilliant artistic partnership and also excelled individually as maritime artists. Their work was informed by first-hand seafaring experience and the Elder had been present at some of the actions of the Anglo-Dutch wars as an official war artist. These experiences, in tandem with their artistic talent, helped to introduce a greater fidelity and realism into the genre of maritime art in Britain. Wilkinson's interest in the van de Veldes almost certainly encouraged him to later donate his series of Second World War oil paintings, entitled the 'War at Sea', which included actions and incidents that he had witnessed, to the National Maritime Museum, Greenwich.

Some of Wilkinson's earliest work was obtained through his doctor, Arthur Conan Doyle, the celebrated author of Sherlock Holmes, who worked for a time as a general practitioner in Southsea. Doyle provided references for Wilkinson to meet author Jerome K. Jerome, famous for *Three Men in a Boat* (1889) and *Three Men on the Bummel* (1900), who was based in London, where he published the *Idler* and *Today*. Wilkinson produced several illustrations for both magazines.

Portrait of Arthur Conan Doyle. Library of Congress.

In March 1898 Wilkinson's depiction of the Royal Yacht at night in Portsmouth Harbour guarded by picket-boats was accepted and published as his first submission for the *Illustrated London News* (*ILN*). It was the start of a long and rewarding relationship. The *ILN* sent him on several overseas assignments, most notably as their special artist in New York to cover Sir Thomas Lipton's challenge to win the America's Cup with *Shamrock II* in 1901 against the defender *Columbia*. Co-owned by the American banker, financier and art collector J.P. Morgan, *Columbia* won all three races. In addition, Wilkinson was sent in 1904 to make drawings at the German kaiser's International Yachting Regatta at Kiel. The roving visual artist noted that 'The Emperor had determined that Germany should be put on the map as a yachting nation'.

Eager to acquire more seafaring experience, Wilkinson sailed in coastal colliers and fishing trawlers around Britain – and further afield in the tramp steamer *Ben Nevis* to Barcelona and Antwerp before returning home. During this time he 'produced a wealth of sketches, some on canvas, but many in that store-house of pictures, the brain'. Determined to make longer passages to more exotic locations, he approached shipping companies with the offer of poster designs in exchange for a passage. One notable arrangement was

agreed with the Booth Line, with the artist sailing on SS *Cyril* to South America where he was particularly taken with Manaus (Manaós), the capital city of the state of Amazonas in northern Brazil. He recalled: 'Manaus is one of the most surprising cities … a thousand miles up the river, entirely surrounded by dense jungle for hundreds of miles. The city has electric light, electric trams, one of the largest Opera Houses in the world, a Cathedral, hotels, in fact all the amenities of a European town.'

Wilkinson in later life, through professional civilian projects and for personal pleasure, was able to explore and paint parts of Abadan, a city in and the capital of Abadan County, Khuzestan, Iran; the Bahamas; Hudson Bay in northeastern Canada; Malta; and Venice.

In addition to steamships, Wilkinson was fascinated by ocean liners. With his close friend and fellow artist Cecil George Charles King (1881–1942), who would also become a significant contributor to the Dazzle painting scheme, they saw the RMS *Titanic* on the morning of 10 April 1912 in Southampton. The ship would sail on her tragic maiden voyage that afternoon. Wilkinson had met Captain Edward Smith before, so both he and King were welcomed aboard and able to look around the ship. Wilkinson's earlier meeting with the captain related to the creation of two of his oil paintings, one apiece for the elegant First Class Smoke Rooms of the White Star Line's sister ships RMS *Olympic* and RMS *Titanic*, entitled *The Approach to the New World* and *Plymouth Harbour*. The painting *Plymouth Harbour* was lost with the *Titanic*; however, Rodney Norman Wilkinson, MC (the son of Norman, who followed his father's profession) re-created it for the SeaCity Museum, Southampton. Norman Wilkinson's original painting for the *Olympic* has survived and is also on display at the same museum.

The paintings were recorded in Wilkinson's work ledger as having sold for a total of 350 guineas and were commissioned by William Pirrie, 1st Viscount Pirrie, the Chairman of the Belfast shipbuilders Harland and Wolff, the company that built the *Olympic*-class vessels. Wilkinson kept meticulous working records, which are still in the possession of descendants of the artist. Lord Pirrie later provided a 'reference' for Wilkinson, albeit one that was not officially authorized, that assisted him during the claims and counter-claims relating to the post-war Dazzle painting 'prize'. Glyn L. Evans observes in *Dazzle-Painted Ships of World War I* (2015) that Wilkinson had picked out the pertinent lines from a letter received from Lord Pirrie in December 1918

Norman Wilkinson The Approach to the New World, *oil on canvas. Southampton City Council Arts & Heritage.*

thanking him for his Christmas card. He wrote: 'I think the various designs you have brought out for the ships have been excellent and I am sure the splendid work you have been doing has safeguarded hundreds of lives and ships.' Lord Pirrie almost certainly approved of Wilkinson's initiative.

Wilkinson's network of influence reached new heights post-war. In August 1919 he was elected as Honorary Painter to the Royal Yacht Squadron, although he admitted that 'he had never had the good fortune to own a racing yacht'. Instead, he owned a Falmouth Quay Punt of 12 tons that he called *Wild Rose*. Purchased in

1911, he said of her, 'I do not know a more weatherly and comfortable type of vessel'. However, the artist crewed for many owners and was paid to paint some of the finest vessels afloat.

During Cowes Week of 1921 he witnessed the royal yacht *Britannia* racing off the Hampshire coast with King George V aboard. He worked up the painting in his London studio from sketches and drawings made on the spot. The artist observed: 'As she came to a level keel on rounding the buoy we could see that her decks were well awash and that H.M. the King was racing in her with the water up to the top of his sea boots.'

In 1922 this large painting, measuring approximately 60in by 80in (153cm by 203cm), was exhibited at the Royal Academy of Arts with the title *HM Yacht Britannia rounding Lymington Spit Buoy in a squall*, although the title was changed to *Britannia passing the East Lepe buoy, Solent, 1921*. It was later purchased by a syndicate of yachtsmen and presented to the king.

On 4 August 1923 Wilkinson was invited to attend the presentation aboard the steam yacht *Victoria and Albert III* at Cowes, and although pleased with the picture the king requested that the artist make a significant change to depict the yacht in a more positive

LONDON BY LMS
ST. PAUL'S CATHEDRAL
NORMAN WILKINSON, P.R.I.

light. Wilkinson had met the king before, during his visit in 1917 to the Dazzle Section at Burlington House, London. The king said: 'The facts are as you have painted them ... but don't you think for the sake of posterity it would look better if we were making a little tighter turn round the buoy? Do you think you could put the buoy a little nearer to the ship?' Wilkinson responded diplomatically: 'Certainly Sir, I can do that in a few minutes.' Since 1984 the painting has been on long-term loan from the Royal Collection to the Royal Yacht Squadron, Cowes. Wilkinson was later also appointed Honorary Marine Painter to the Royal

Norman Wilkinson, London by LMS, *1925 poster. Getty Images.*

Thames Yacht Club.

Although extremely well connected, and now enjoying royal approval, Wilkinson tried unsuccessfully to gain membership of the Royal Academy of Arts (RA), or Royal Academy, an organization that had been formally established in 1768. His rejection related to the restricted membership (limited to 40 full RA members) of that society and the long-standing presence there of the venerated marine artist William Lionel Wyllie RA (1851–1931), who in 1869 had been awarded the RA Schools Turner Gold Medal and was elected a full member of the RA in 1907. This did not deter Wilkinson from submitting works for their annual summer exhibition on a regular and long-standing basis. In 1903 he exhibited his first painting, entitled *In touch with the enemy; naval manoeuvres*, and his last in 1970, the year before his death. However, the art society with which Wilkinson had the most intimate association was the Royal Institute of Painters in Water Colours (RI) that was originally established in 1831. He became a member in 1906 and was elected president from 1936, an appointment he held until 1963.

Wilkinson was also a member of the Royal Institute of Oil Painters (ROI). He was associated with the Royal Society of British Artists (RBA), the Royal Scottish Society of Painters in Watercolour (RSW) and became president of the Wapping Group of Artists. In 1939 he was a founder-member of the Society of Marine Artists, later given the prefix Royal.

A clubbable man, Wilkinson was a regular at the St. John's Wood Arts Club and was closely connected with, or a guest member of, several others – notably the Chelsea Arts Club, the Savage Club, the London Sketch Club and the Arts Club in Dover Street. At the St. John's Wood Arts Club, Wilkinson shared membership with Charles William Wyllie (1853–1923), the brother of the eminent marine artist William Lionel Wyllie, RA. Charles was also enlisted by Wilkinson to assist with the Dazzle painting of ships. The club provided him with an eclectic group of friends and acquaintances that included the composer George Frederic Norton (1860–1946) and Francis Barraud (1856–1924) who in 1899 had painted the hugely popular picture *His Master's Voice* in which the Jack Russell Terrier Nipper was depicted listening to the cylinder phonograph; E.J. (Edwin John) Odell (1835–1928) the comedian and actor, although it was so long ago no one could remember him on the stage; Arthur Rackham (1867–1939), one of the leading figures in the 'Golden Age' of British book illustration; Samuel John 'Lamorna' Birch, RA, RWS (1869–1955), who was associated with the Newlyn and Lamorna schools of art; and Adrian Stokes, RA, who Wilkinson had first met during his visits to St. Ives, was 'one of our most lovable of characters'.

Norman Wilkinson's subjects were wide ranging. In addition to marine subjects, they included landscapes, cityscapes, trains and planes. He was a keen fly-fisherman, a passion shared with 'Lamorna' Birch, and produced many angling subjects in painted, printed and published formats. In addition, his poster designs for railway companies were innovative and in high demand. He advocated 'simplicity and truth' in his designs, which the poster specialist Paul Rennie has observed broke with the existing practice of complex and detailed images.

One of his earliest poster designs was produced for the London and North Western Railway Company (LNWR) in 1905, which he described as 'a forerunner of the artistic railway poster'. The artist later claimed that he was 'the originator of the modern pictorial poster'. Glyn L. Evans has suggested that the use of 'blocks of bold colour' in Wilkinson's posters had an impact on the development of his Dazzle painting concept.

Insights into the circles in which Wilkinson moved, with regard to his poster designs and commercial work, can be found in a lecture attended by the artist at the Royal Society of Arts in John Adam Street, London, that was published in its journal on 23 January 1914. W.S. Rogers' presentation was entitled 'The Modern Poster: Its Essentials and Significance'. The lecture was chaired by John Hassall, popularly known as the 'King of the Posters' and still best known for his image of the fat jolly fisherman skipping along a strip of Lincolnshire beach in the poster *Skegness is So Bracing*, originally designed for the Great Northern Railway (GNR) in 1908; and his recruitment designs for public schools in the First World War. Other attendees included Joseph Pennell, the American artist, author and friend of Whistler; Tony Sarg, the German-American puppeteer and illustrator; and Bert Thomas, the brilliant social cartoonist who had a long working relationship with *London Opinion* magazine and produced propaganda posters in the both world wars.

During the questions afterwards Wilkinson articulated his view on the challenges then being faced in the production of posters in Britain. He thought that 'British posters suffered from their great number, a good one being to a certain extent lost among several bad ones' and that 'some advertisers considered that a decision on the question of an advertisement could be left to a few off moments, when business was finished, and did not require any particular knowledge; while such an attitude obtained [he stressed], poor posters will be produced'.

In 1924 Wilkinson acted as an art-advisor on posters in the advertising department of the London, Midland and Scottish Railway (LMS). In his quest to raise the standard of British poster design he enlisted many of the leading artists of the RA. He used his formidable charm and persuasion to ensure that 17 out of the 18 artists, a mix of RAs and ARAs at that time (the latter included Algernon Talmage, ARA), completed their designs for the sum of £100. Sir David Young Cameron, RA, and Sir David Murray, RA, produced *The Scottish Highlands* and *Conway* respectively; Sir William Orpen, RA, and Richard Jack, RA, contributed *The Night Mail* and *British Industries*; while Norman Wilkinson completed *Grangemouth Docks*. Wilkinson was the only artist outside of the RA. Leonard Campbell Taylor, ARA, also contributed a poster design. Earlier he had been selected by Wilkinson to work in the Dazzle Section at the RA.

Wilkinson contributed a poster to the Empire Marketing Board (EMB), the organization established in May 1926 to promote 'intra-Empire trade' and persuade consumers to 'buy Empire'. His successful submission was entitled *Ships in the Channel* and was placed in the

A FEW CARELESS WORDS MAY END IN THIS—

Many lives were lost in the last war through careless talk
Be on your guard! Don't discuss movements of ships or troops

EMB's category 'Scenes of Marketing'. On 2 November 1926 a selection of the original artworks for the posters was held at the RA. Among the other marine painters who contributed to the EMB were Charles Dixon and Charles Pears (1873–1958), the latter was the first president of the Society of Marine Painters and an official war artist in both world wars. Although he was not officially part of Wilkinson's Dazzle Section he produced some of the most striking oil paintings of Dazzled ships. They include *Dazzled: A Camouflaged Battleship HMS 'Ramillies' in a gale of wind* (1918) [page 11], *HMS 'Fearless'* (1918)[page 81], *A Dazzled Merchantman* (1918) [pages 4–5] and *A view of the aircraft carrier HMS 'Furious' at sea* (1919).

During the Second World War Wilkinson contributed a memorable poster for the government's anti-rumour/gossip campaign that depicted a sinking ship with the slogan 'A Few Careless Words May End In This'. He also worked for the British Air Ministry and was given the challenging brief to conceal airfields from enemy bombardment. In addition, Wilkinson also produced Dazzle designs for aircraft. One example of an 'Aeroplane Scout' can be seen in the RAF Museum. Remarkably, after his retirement from the Royal Air Force as Inspector of Camouflage before the end of the war, he turned his attention to the creation of a large series of oil paintings collectively entitled *The War at Sea*, of which Wilkinson noted: 'The numbers grew, until I had completed 56 pictures'.

The National Gallery (NG) in London exhibited 54 of the paintings in 1944, and at that time he presented them to the War Artists Advisory Committee. The paintings were later transferred to the National Maritime Museum, Greenwich, after their first exhibition there on 22 June 1950, which was opened by Lord Mountbatten.

In the introduction to the NG's exhibition catalogue, Admiral of the Fleet Andrew Browne Cunningham, 1st Viscount Cunningham of Hyndhope, wrote that the paintings: '...present two and a half years work and range over the work of the Navy, the Merchant Navy and Coastal Command, all partners in the war at sea.' Also, that: '...the public will be no less anxious than the Navy to enjoy the pictures and pay tribute to their superb artistry and to the generosity of the artist. I sincerely hope they will be shown and appreciated widely both at home and in the Empire overseas.'

THE WAR AT SEA

LD 4291 *The Road to Normandy.*

A Series of pictures painted by Norman Wilkinson, O.B.E., P.R.I., and presented by him to the War Artists Advisory Committee.

NATIONAL GALLERY

invasion on D-Day, and on a number of subsequent days, in the destroyer *Jervis*, one of the war's veterans. Sketching in a destroyer in action is not too easy; so much is going on it is difficult to concentrate on one incident. It therefore becomes a matter of rapid shorthand notes until a moment comes when the notes can be elaborated in colour and in more detail.'

Dazzle painting had reached its apogee in 1918. It was not used again in the Second World War on a wide scale. Dazzle evolved into disruptive camouflage, the umbrella name for various painting schemes that can be linked to Dazzle but were visually far less sensational. Disruptive camouflage can be seen in Wilkinson's *Landing Craft going to the beaches, 6th June 1944* on the *Jervis*, the large vessel left of centre in the composition.

Norman Wilkinson was also involved with a number of highly successful art initiatives to raise money for naval charities. His extensive achievements were given royal approval with his awards of Officer of the Most Excellent Order of the British Empire (OBE) in 1918 in recognition of his Dazzle painting work and Commander *of the Most Excellent Order of the British Empire* (CBE) in 1948.

To create his Dazzle painting scheme, Wilkinson drew upon his extensive artistic and seafaring skills and experience, as well as his adeptness at promotional publicity and networking. In order to comprehend his scheme and understand what he hoped it would achieve, we need to return to the time of Wilkinson's enlistment in the Royal Navy to scrutinise key parts of his service record and artistic creations in the First World War when the idea first occurred.

Wilkinson also contributed to the catalogue with 'A Note by the Artist' in which he revealed: 'The pictures have been painted from many sources, those showing Naval actions being reconstructed from descriptions supplied by participants in the actions concerned. It is difficult for a single member of a ship's company to give a comprehensive idea of a Naval action in which he is engaged. Funnel smoke and gunfire may at times completely mask the field of vision of one observer, while in another vessel an observer may be so placed as to see this area clearly. I have therefore tried to build up the pictures from a number of independent and authentic sources. As a result, it has been found that in the main one has been able to satisfy those engaged in the actions that the pictures do give a reasonably true impression of the events portrayed.'

He went on to explain that he was present during one major event and highlighted the challenges of the working conditions aboard ship to create a good composition: 'I was fortunate in being present at the

(opposite) Norman Wilkinson, A Few Careless Words May End In This, poster, printed by Greycaine Ltd., Watford and London. Imperial War Musuem (PST 13957).

(above) Cover of 'The War At Sea' catalogue featuring Wilkinson's series of Second World War marine paintings first exhibited at the National Gallery, London in August 1944.

(overleaf) Norman Wilkinson, Landing Craft going to the beaches, 6th June 1944, oil on canvas, (note camouflage on the destroyer Jervis *left of centre in the composition). National Maritime Museum, Greenwich, London.*

NORMAN WILKINSON
PAINTED FROM SKETCHES MADE
AT THE NORMANDY LANDING
JUNE 6TH 1944

THE DAZZLE PAINTING CONCEPT

E arly in 1915 Wilkinson, then in his mid-30s, felt compelled that he 'must get into the Navy'. After passing a perfunctory 'fit for duty test' at Portsmouth, and through the assistance of Captain Halton Stirling Lecky, he was commissioned as an assistant paymaster Royal Naval Reserve (RNR). Sailing aboard several vessels he would eventually arrive in the Dardanelles.

On arrival at the town of Moudros on the island of Lemnos, Greece, he was questioned by Admiral Arthur Henry Christian. Wilkinson reported that Christian said, 'I had no idea you were an artist. I shan't have much for you to do so you had better spend some of your time making sketches of operations'. Wilkinson noted that from that time he was 'given a completely free hand to go where I liked'.

During this period he rapidly produced many striking sketches and drawings and evocative watercolours, some of which he later developed into oil paintings of his day-to-day observations and first-hand records of the incidents and actions. Two of his best-known oils are *The Base Camp, Cape Helles, under Shell Fire, August 1915: The SS 'River Clyde' Aground* and *Troops Landing on C Beach, Suvla Bay, Later in the Day, 7 August 1915*. They were both painted in 1919 but first appeared in *The Dardanelles – Colour Sketches from Gallipoli* 'written and drawn' by Wilkinson and published by Longmans, Green and Co. in 1915. The original artworks are in the Imperial War Museum.

Wilkinson served in Gibraltar on submarine patrol as assistant paymaster RNR and then as paymaster aboard the armed yacht *Valiant II* – the vessel that brought him back to Britain with the new rank of Lieutenant RNVR (Royal Naval Volunteer Reserve). In 1917 Wilkinson recalled he was posted to the Devonport Naval Barracks and his first assignment was on 'one of the 80-foot motor launches' and 'with a companion ship, we were the first

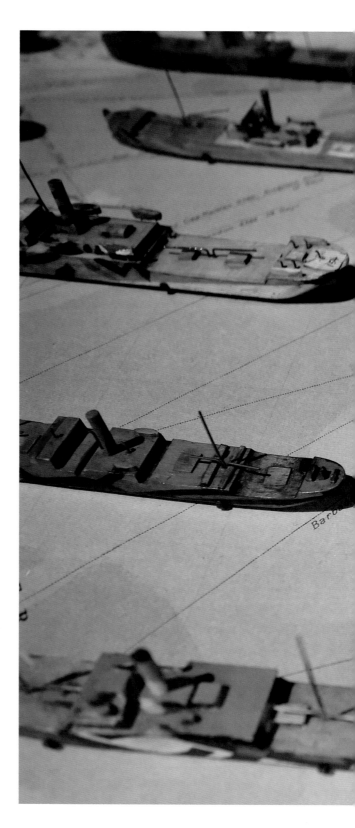

A selection of Dazzled ship models used by Norman Wilkinson and his team in the Dazzle Section at Burlington House. Getty Images.

to be fitted for mine-sweeping'. It was at this time that Wilkinson developed his Dazzle painting idea.

Germany's introduction of unrestricted submarine warfare in February 1915 was short-lived. The sinking of the Cunarder *Lusitania* close to the Old Head of Kinsale in Ireland on 7 May 1915 with the loss of around 1,200 lives, including 128 American citizens, proved counter-productive to the Germans. It was one of the key events that eventually led to the USA entering the war in support of Britain and her allies as an associate power in early April 1917. This tragic incident was captured by Wilkinson in a dramatic watercolour reproduced in black-and-white in the *Illustrated London News*.

In January 1917, frustrated by the resolute resistance to her imperial ambitions and goals, Germany reintroduced unrestricted submarine warfare. From March to December 1917 the German campaign against British and Allied shipping came close to cutting off all vital supplies and starving Britain into submission. Amanda Mason of the Imperial War Museum in her online article titled 'The U-Boat Campaign That Almost Broke Britain' reveals that 'between February and April 1917, U-boats sank more than 500 merchant ships. In the second half of April, an average of 13 ships were sunk each day.' In the same month, although the specific figures were unknown to him, Wilkinson sent a formal offer of assistance to the Admiralty outlining his Dazzle

painting idea to protect British merchant shipping. It was a perfectly timed approach.

During his minesweeping duties between Start Point in Devon and Portland Bill, the southernmost point of Dorset, Wilkinson observed: '...we frequently saw vessels, sometimes in company, and what I particularly noticed was that in most cases Admiralty transports were painted black, which seemed to me to be asking for trouble as a submarine Commander could wish for no better target than a black ship, by day or night.'

It was on the return from a weekend fishing trip that the idea for Dazzle painting came to Wilkinson. He wrote: 'On my way back to Devonport in the early morning, in an extremely cold carriage, I suddenly got the idea that since it was impossible to paint a ship so that she could not be seen by a submarine, the extreme opposite was the answer – in other words, to paint her, not for low visibility, but in such a way as to break up her form and thus confuse a submarine officer as to the course on which she was heading.'

Immediately on his return to barracks he met with the commander to convey his idea by way of a 'rough draft of a camouflaged ship to my own ideas, showing port and starboard side'. After the commander's agreement, Wilkinson then set about arranging a meeting with Captain Charles Frederick Thorp, who was in charge of the dockyard. Thorp

(left) Norman Wilkinson, Troops Landing on C beach, Sulva Bay, Later in the Day, 7 August 1915, *oil on canvas. Imperial War Museum (ART 2452). This painting derives from Wilkinson's earlier watercolour.*

(opposite top) W E T (signed with initials although artist unknown) World War I recruitment poster Irishmen Avenge The Lusitania *poster printed by John Shuley and Co, Dublin in May 1915. Library of Congress.*

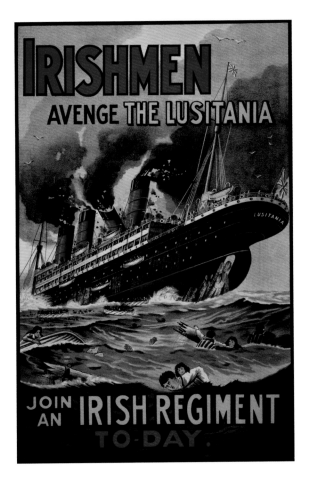

2. *The proposal is to paint a ship with large patches of strong colour in a carefully thought out pattern and colour scheme, which will so distort the form of the vessel that chances of successful aim by attacking Submarines will be greatly decreased.*

3. *The accompanying diagrams, selected at random, are intended to illustrate the scheme.*

4. *Attention is specially directed to the size and proportion of the colour patches. This is a most important point, as if the pattern is too small, the result is negligible at a distance at which Submarines usually operate.*

5. *Earlier theories for the disguising of seagoing ships have been confined almost entirely to War Vessels, and have had invisibility for their aim, whereas in this case, it should be pointed out, the idea is not to render the ship in any degree invisible, as this is virtually impossible, but to largely distort the external shape by means of violent contrasts.*

6. *At present, the average Merchant Ship, with her all black or all grey hull, offers [an] ideal target, and shows the enemy Submarine her shape and length exactly, whereas by the scheme proposed she must, at least, present more of a problem to the attacker and confuse his judgment as to her proportions, and so enormously diminish the chance of the vessels being struck.*

7. *The diagrams submitted herewith are only a very small selection of innumerable patterns that can be evolved, and are merely intended to give a general idea of what is aimed at. But were the opportunity afforded to experiment, it is believed that considerable progress could be achieved with the idea.*

8. *Other features of the scheme worth considering are, the cheapness and rapidity with which it could be carried out, practically nothing in the way of material being required beyond what is ready to hand. While a further strong point which I would submit to your notice is the infinite variety of designs evolvable, so that no design need ever be used twice, and Submarine Commanders would never become accustomed to the appearance of ships.*

was suffering from fatigue and initially reluctant to see Wilkinson, however he eventually consented. Wilkinson's persuasive personality won through and the commander warmed to the idea. It was concluded that he should work with Thorp's naval secretary to develop a proposal to include a 'rough sketch of a ship to illustrate the scheme' to be forwarded to the Admiralty for consideration. Meanwhile, Wilkinson returned to his minesweeping duties.

On 27 April 1917 Wilkinson sent his letter proposal (below) in point-form to the Admiralty. Coincidentally, it was also the same day that the convoy system was introduced in an attempt to protect shipping.

Sir, I have the honour to submit the following ideas for the protection of Merchant Shipping and 'Q' boats [merchant ships with hidden weapons used to destroy submarines] from Submarine attack by torpedoes.

Developing point five of Wilkinson's proposal, not only was it impossible to make a ship invisible but the U-boat had the means to establish the presence of a vessel through the noise of her engines by using hydrophones and by the sight of emissions of smoke from her funnels. The U-boat had to come close to the surface to utilize her periscope in order to estimate the ship's type, course and speed. To achieve this she only had a short period of time (often less than a minute) before the submarine's wake would reveal her presence to the vessel being hunted. Wilkinson's Dazzle painting scheme aimed 'to largely distort the external shape by means of violent contrasts' so as to confuse the submarine commander. It was hoped to achieve one of three outcomes: to force the attacker to abandon the strike; to misdirect the torpedo away from the vessel; or to misdirect it to a less vulnerable part of the ship, enabling it to escape or possibly fight back. Wilkinson never promised that his scheme offered immunity from attack.

After a fortnight Wilkinson was frustrated at the lack of response and so he wrote to an influential acquaintance at the Admiralty, Rear Admiral Clement Greatorex, Director of Naval Equipment (DNE). On 29 May Wilkinson received his reply: 'Your "scheme" was delayed owing to passing through several Departments, but I was able to get hold of it and took immediate action to have the "Industry" selected in the manner you are aware of. I see no necessity for you coming to Admiralty to discuss the scheme. It is decentralised to be in the hands of Devonport, and the Flag Captain can make all arrangements for what is required – you to see him as to details.'

Greatorex added: 'It appears to me that you might like to paint your ship differently one side to the other.' This was adopted as standard practice.

Matters were well advanced, as evidenced by the letter marked 'Secret' written in point-form and sent to Wilkinson on 23 May from R.R. Scott, secretary to the Admiralty. He wrote:

With reference to your submission of the Admiralty, of 28th April No.1011/6, I am commanded by My Lords Commissioners of the Admiralty to acquaint you in confirmation of Admiralty telegram of today's date that the Store Ship 'Industry' is to be painted in accordance with the proposals of Lieutenant Wilkinson R.N.V.R. of M.L./193. This officer should be directed to consult with the Flag Captain, Devonport, as to the exact method of painting, following the proposals forwarded with your submission. It is desired that all arrangements for painting should be made forthwith in order that the ship may not be delayed longer than possible.

After repainting, the *Industry* sailed on her regular route, calling at Chatham, Portsmouth, Plymouth, Pembroke and Queenstown. Painting the vessel with Dazzle paint was one thing, but how would the Admiralty know if the scheme actually worked? Scott answered this question in point two of his letter:

2. I am also to state that the Admiral Superintendent Devonport, should, forward to the Admiralty the details of the scheme of painting adopted for inclusion in Confidential Interim Orders in order that reports may be forwarded by Coast Stations, Ships, and Submarines which may sight the Ships when at sea in all weathers and varying conditions.

Wilkinson pointed out in his autobiography that he was troubled by this order to report on the effectiveness of the Dazzle-painted *Industry*. He wrote: '...a ship seen from the shore and other ships was not the point of view for which I painted her. The sole idea of this particular form of painting was protection against submarine

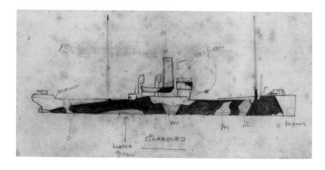

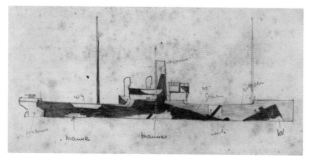

(above) Norman Wilkinson drawings of the port and starboard sides of the store ship Industry. *Wilkinson Estate.*

attack. The submarine's point of view, would be a few inches above the surface of the sea, the ship being seen against the sky with little sea foreground.'

After meeting with Greatorex in London it was made clear to Wilkinson that his scheme would not be widely adopted until sufficient reports had confirmed its veracity. Also, that if adopted there was no room in any of the Admiralty buildings and so he would have to use his own initiative and endeavours to secure a suitable location to undertake the required work.

Anticipating positive feedback about the scheme, he was successful with the backing of Sir Edward Poynter, president of the Royal Academy of Arts, to secure space in one of the studio rooms in the RA Schools, where they taught the art students. This was confirmed in writing by the secretary, W.R.M. Lamb, on 16 June 1917.

Frustrated with the delays in receiving feedback from the Admiralty and wanting to speed things up, Wilkinson sought assistance from a friend in the Ministry of Shipping, then based in St. James's Park, London. The friend is not named, but he promised to raise the matter at an important committee meeting of prominent shipowners in the presence of the chairman, Sir Joseph Paton Maclay, 1st Baronet. This resulted in Wilkinson being asked to present his scheme to the committee, which he illustrated with 'some pencil drawings...made on the spot'. Wilkinson noted that they 'grasped the idea immediately, which was certainly novel from the point of view of camouflage as hitherto accepted'.

Lord Maclay was eager to introduce the scheme immediately, although Wilkinson correctly anticipated that Greatorex would be furious with his manoeuvring. He was summoned to Greatorex's office and according to Wilkinson: '...we had a ding-dong row and I finally walked out.'

The Dazzle painting scheme was approved before the official trial reports had returned. Interestingly, after the reports had come in they were encouraging, although

Portrait of Sir Joseph Paton Maclay.

far from being overwhelming positive. However, in Wilkinson's defence, his scheme was created with the purpose of confusing an enemy submarine and not a ship at sea or guns ashore. The results were as follows: '(a) From Ships at sea. Favourable 27. Indifferent 14. Unfavourable 5. (b) From War Signal Stations. Favourable 26. Indifferent 33. Unfavourable 12.'

The overall control of the Dazzle Section, as it became known, would later be transferred from Rear Admiral Greatorex, Director of Naval Equipment (DNE), to the Controller of Merchant Shipbuilding, although in the initial stages Greatorex was still actively involved. Fortunately for Wilkinson, Greatorex was promoted and his role as DNE was taken over, on 8 October 1917, by Rear Admiral Edward Montgomery Phillpotts until the end of the war. However, Professor John Graham Kerr recollected – in his planned but abandoned autobiography *War Paint* – that it was Admiral Greatorex who invented the word Dazzle and that, 'The word was chosen for the purpose of contrasting it with camouflage'.

Wilkinson was officially transferred to the DNE 'Dazzle Section' in June 1917 and by 1 September he was granted a consolidated salary of £600 per annum as operations manager, with a technical allowance of 5 shillings a day until 12 November of that year. At the outset he tried to obtain promotion to lieutenant commander, and although this was initially refused he was promoted a few months later on 20 December. Wilkinson was both the operations manager and creative director. He recollected that it was initially a challenge to find suitable staff, although he did have some useful contacts who were enlisted and made lieutenants RNVR. Eventually, 'a staff of about twenty girls, all of whom had been selected because they have been to art schools' were appointed. And: 'Amongst the men...I got a number who could make models of ships. These models, on average about a foot long, represented every type of merchant ship that it might be necessary to camouflage. Wooden models were then made with flat bottoms. The model was now painted to a particular scheme of camouflage.'

Initially, the staff comprised of 'five Lieutenants R.N.V.R who designed the schemes of "Dazzle" painting, three modellers, two men and one woman who constructed models to scale of all ships painted and Lady Clerks for colouring plans of ships'.

As the workload of the Dazzle Section increased and the staff expanded, more space was required. The RA's annual report for 1917 noted: 'In June the Council were approached by the Director of Naval Equipment, Admiralty for the loan of a studio in which to conduct painting experiments in the disguise of ships at sea, and the permission was readily given.' By September of that year it is known from a later RA report that the Admiralty was making use of five spaces normally occupied by the RA Schools. Wilkinson recollected:

I borrowed a periscope from the Admiralty [and] this

Two interior photographs of Dazzle section of Burlington House. The ship models were Dazzle painted predominantly by women and then tested in the theatre using a persicope. Wilkinson Estate.

was erected at one end of a long table. About 7 feet from the periscope, a circular table was then cut out which could be slowly turned by a handle near the periscope. In this way one could judge the maximum distortion one was trying to achieve in order to upset a submarine Commander's idea of the particular course on which the ship was moving. The model was then handed to one of my girl assistants, who, on a white paper plan [1-16 inch scale] of the particular type of ship concerned, coloured in accordance with the colours on the model.

Wilkinson stressed that this stage was essential for the success of the scheme as 'each colour on the plan was numbered to conform to the official colour charts, which gave a complete range of all colours used in dazzle painting'. The chart accompanied the entry on 'Naval Camouflage' that Norman Wilkinson wrote for the 11th edition of the *Encyclopaedia Britannica* (vol.xxix, 1922). It was, in his estimation, 'one of the most important factors essential to the success of the scheme that these colours should be rigidly adhered to by painting contractors'.

Jan Gordon (whose real name was Godfrey Jervis Gordon) served as a Dazzle Officer under Wilkinson, and he provides some additional details of the process in his article 'The Art of Dazzle-Painting' that was published in *Land & Water* magazine on 12 December 1918. He wrote:

These types [of ships] were modelled in wood about nine to twelve inches length by three expert model makers. The models were then Dazzled by the designers and tested in the theatre. This theatre consisted of a long sea-tinted platform in which were let turntables at various ranges, and at the back a canvas screen painted to approximate a normal sky value. At the observing end of the table a periscope permitted observations to be made as if from an actual submarine, and from the length of model and the distance of the turntable ranges were calculated. The model was tested, altered, tested again upon various bearings, till it was judged that a maximum amount of distortion and disguise had been produced, and then from the model transferred to a type plan by a large staff of lady artists. From the type plan the painting was carried out on the actual ship. In the case of special ships, special models had to be made.

Gordon also recollected: 'It would obviously be impossible to make a separate design for every one of the ships trading in the English mercantile marine, so they have been divided into a number of types— the type dependent upon certain marked differences in construction and length. These types covered more or less any variation of ship which could be found, and the dazzle officers at the various centres fitted these plans to the ships which came beneath their control.'

In addition to the port and starboard sides of each ship featured on the plans, some also included details of the Dazzle designs for the funnels, bridge, bow and stern.

Sets of plans were then sent to Wilkinson's supervisors in key ports around Britain and they were tasked to adapt them for the selected vessels. After the gradual closure of the Dazzle Section between January and May 1919 (Wilkinson was demobilized in May, although he had been moved on to other painting projects for the Royal Navy and Imperial War Museum) most of the plans and models were transferred to the Imperial War Museum, where some of the latter can be seen on display in the new museum café and restaurant. A small number were left behind at Burlington House, the home of the RA, after the Dazzle Section had vacated the rooms. To coincide with the First World War centenary commemorations they were placed on public display in the RA Library Print Room from 14 October 2014 to 30 January 2015.

The mix of designs on the models and plans is visually overwhelming. Violently contrasting colours contained within arcing, curving, sloping, diagonal and zig-zag lines mixed with saw-tooth patterns, also vessels with black-and-white zebra-like stripes and tiger-like markings all compete for attention.

The development of the Dazzle designs was driven in part by the testing of the models in the miniature theatre at Burlington House and also by trial and error. A number of key principles were gradually established in terms of the execution of the designs. The military historian Guy Hartcup, in *Camouflage – A History of Concealment and Deception in War* (1979), has summarized the main ones:

The light parts of the design were painted with two light colours, each with a distinctive tone. The reason for this was that there was a better chance of one colour harmonising with the sky behind; it helped to distort the ship when used in conjunction with black and dark greys. …

… The most important parts of the ship to distort were those near the stern and the fore-bridge, both useful for the submarine in determining the course of its proposed victim. The bow end on the starboard side might be painted white and the after end a shade of blue. These colours would be reversed on the port side. It was important that a colour should not be allowed to stop at and therefore define important constructional details such as the stern, or the centre of the centre of the stern. Thus either the white on the starboard side or the blue on the port side had to be carried round the stern, until checked by part of the dark pattern; the same had to be done for the bow-end.

In Archibald Hurd's chapter on 'Dazzle Painting' in *History of the Great War – The Merchant Navy* (Vol.III, 1924), he draws upon the official Admiralty archives to note the three key ways in which Wilkinson's scheme was applied to ships to afford protection:

Breaking up the surface of a ship by the use of violently contrasting pigments; Painting the bow so that its sharp edge appeared to be moved several feet to the side; & Providing wide strips of different colours, carried up from the hull over superstructure, funnels, bridge, and boats, thus creating such a medley that a submarine commander at the periscope should be at a loss to know upon what particular part of a ship he was sighting.

Hurd also recorded that:

In the earlier stages of dazzle painting, the practice was to use large black masses with drab or coloured intervals and in the course of development experiments were made with vivid colourings, red being the most conspicuous. These, however, proved to be less satisfactory, and after a few months were abandoned, and the standard colours became black, white, grey, and various shades of blue and green, one object of the blue and green being to make the lighter parts of the ship melt into the sky at different periods of the day. The first considerable advance in dazzle painting resulted from the adoption of stripe patterns. These, when first used experimentally, were not sufficiently heavy to counteract the solidity of the ship, but with the employment of large and bold designs,

Merchant vessel dazzle-painted as seen through a submarine periscope.

The same vessel on identical course painted grey.

Standard ship.

Patrol sloop.

Two ideal types of ships specially designed and dazzle-painted for protection against submarine attack.

General appearance of a dazzle-painted convoy at sea.

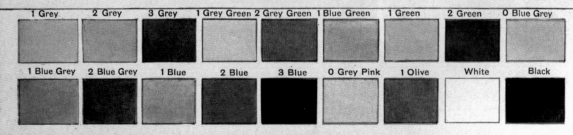

1 Grey	2 Grey	3 Grey	1 Grey Green	2 Grey Green	1 Blue Green	1 Green	2 Green	0 Blue Grey
1 Blue Grey	2 Blue Grey	1 Blue	2 Blue	3 Blue	0 Grey Pink	1 Olive	White	Black

Colour chart issued to painting contractors showing the principal colours used in dazzle-painting.

(opposite) Norman Wilkinson's entry on 'Naval Camouflage' in the 11th edition of the Encyclopaedia Britannica, *vol. xxix, 1922.*

One of the Imperial War Museum's small Dazzle hand-painted ship models –Type 17 C X – in brown, grey and black (MOD 2464) and a Dazzle hand-drawn port view schematic for the Royal Navy 'Monmouth' class cruisers HMS Cornwall *and HMS* Donegal *(DAZ 00351). These models and plans were used to illustrate the different types of Dazzle. The "Violently contrasting colours contained within arcing, curving, sloping, diagonal and zigzag lines mixed with saw-tooth patterns, also vessels with black and white stripes and tiger-like markings".*

the stripes being carried over the hull and the whole of the upper works, the detail of a ship seen at a long range became greatly confused. Stripes broke up all form more effectively than the big patterns of curves. ... Some of the largest ships afloat were dazzle painted, among them the Cunard liners *Mauretania*, treated with a rising succession of black and light squares to destroy her perspective, and the *Aquitania*, whose enormous hull was covered with stripes, irregular areas, and patches. The American *Leviathan* was also treated.

In the entry by Wilkinson in the *Encyclopaedia Britannica* he noted that: 'In the early stages of dazzle painting a large range of colours was employed to achieve the end in view.' However, '...experience showed that this could be attained by a much smaller number and, towards the end of the war the principal colours in use were black, white and blue, these being employed with various intensity'.

As the war progressed there was a practical reason for the simplification of colours. Neutralizing screens had been adopted by the U-boats to improve range-finding. It worked with multicoloured designs but 'had no effect on a design depending solely on black, white and blue for its contrast'.

Of all the official visitors to the Dazzle Section it was the visit of King George V that gave Wilkinson the greatest pleasure. He arrived on 18 October 1917 accompanied by his equerry, Captain Bryan Godfrey-Fausett, RN. By this time they would have seen 25 women workers in the room where the Dazzle plans were coloured before despatch to the ports. After observing a ship model through the periscope the king was convinced that the ship was heading South by West. Wilkinson informed him that the actual course was East South East, to which the king replied: '...as you know Commander, I have been a professional sailor for many years and I would not have believed I could have been so deceived in my estimate.'

The king wanted him to explain: '...the principle... and...general idea...since the usually accepted notion of Camouflage was that the object to be dealt with was treated in such a way that it was rendered relatively invisible to an enemy, whereas under my scheme a vessel was apparently more visible than ever.'

Wilkinson also recollected the international appeal of Dazzle painting and the training of Allied officers at Burlington House. They included representatives from France, Italy, Japan and Russia. There was less interest in Dazzle painting in the southern hemisphere, with only one vessel, the Town-class light cruiser HMAS

Melbourne (1912), being Dazzled by the Royal Australian Navy during the First World War.

Initially, 50 troopships were painted with different Dazzle designs and the feedback was overwhelmingly positive. Several observers at sea, albeit mainly from ships, found it difficult to work out in which direction the Dazzled vessel was sailing. The Ministry of Shipping was delighted with the results and in October 1917 ordered that all merchant ships in excess of 150 feet in length should be painted with Dazzle designs.

By June 1918 around 2,300 British merchant vessels had been coated in Dazzle paint. However, after Wilkinson's return to work from the U.S., probably in March of that year, Wilkinson had had to overcome a major challenge in relation to his scheme. It started with complaints from the Royal Navy's Mediterranean Fleet relating to the 'white paint...used in contrast to the black was visible on moonlight nights' and ended with an

Admiralty inquiry that was eager to establish the veracity of the Dazzle painting. Cleverly, Wilkinson called upon the assistance of Harold Sanderson, the vice president of the White Star Line, who provided the testimonies of the captains of 50 merchant vessels 'sixty per cent of which were enormously in favour of it and the remainder were either negative or, in a very small number of cases, against it'. The Admiralty decided to continue Dazzle painting.

So just how did Wilkinson's scheme affect the viewer of an enemy submarine? In the absence of detailed feedback from U-boat officers about the effectiveness of the scheme (in fact those captured and questioned claimed it had no effect), there is a lively fictitious account by Henry Newbolt and published in *Submarine and Anti-Submarine* (1918). Newbolt conjures up an imagined scene of the confusion caused by Dazzle-painted ships when viewed through an enemy periscope:

The line, you are told, is not a line at all, but a convoy, in fairly regular formation. The nearest spot is a destroyer, zig-zagging on the flank; the others are ships which have been so effectively 'dazzled' that their shapes are unrecognizable. You carry on, in hope of something nearer, and suddenly a much larger object comes into the fields of vision. A ship, of course, though it does not look like any ship you have ever seen; and you are asked to guess its distance and direction. You are bewildered at first; for as you were moving the lens rapidly to starboard, the vessel came in rapidly to port, and as her dazzle-paint makes her stern indistinguishable from her bows, you continue to think she is steaming in that direction.

He continued:

If you look long and hard at this dazzle-ship. She doesn't give you any sensation of being dazzled; but she is, in some queer way, all wrong...If you fix your attention on one end of her, she seems to point one way – if you look away at her, she is doing something completely different.

And that:

The Commander is interested. He takes a look himself, laughs, and puts you back at the eye-piece...You begin to think that the ingenuity at command of the nation has been underestimated. But this ship is nothing of a

(top) HMAS Melbourne *(1912). The only Australian ship dazzled in Australia during the First World War. Australian War Memorial.*

(above) Norman Wilkinson, Dazzled Ships at Night, *1918, oil on canvas. Imperial War Musuem (ART 4029).*

'Does not look like any ship you have ever seen.'

dazzle, the Commander tells you – he can show you one whose cut-water seems always to be moving at a right angle to her stern!

In this instance because the ship's course could not be accurately determined, it was decided that the submarine should not attack the ship. Newbolt wrote: 'In fact, it would not be worthwhile risking so costly a shot. A torpedo at present prices is worth not far short of £2000, and we only carry two for each tube.'

The book was enhanced by 'a coloured frontispiece and 20 full-page black-and-white illustrations by the marine painter Norman Wilkinson, R.I'. One illustration, entitled *Does not look like any ship you have ever seen*, is placed opposite the key part of the author's text. Although devoid of colour, the image still perfectly demonstrates the visual

confusion created by the effects of Dazzle painting and the difficulty of ascertaining in which direction the ship is actually sailing.

Newbolt's publication is not only fictitious it can be directly linked to the British literary and visual propaganda campaign. At the outset of the war Newbolt had joined Wellington House in London, the headquarters of the British War Propaganda Bureau. He and many other acclaimed authors, poets and editors, who included Arthur Conan Doyle, Thomas Hardy, Jerome K. Jerome, Rudyard Kipling, John Masefield, Sir Own Seaman and H.G. Wells, were tasked to promote Britain's interests and prop up public opinion in favour of it. For his dutiful services, among other things, Newbolt was knighted in 1915.

Wilkinson did not intend his scheme to be associated with morale boosting or propaganda, his primary concern was to utilize his artistic and seafaring skills and experiences for a practical purpose: to diminish the number of British and allied ships that were being targeted and sunk by German U-boats.

Given the extremely high visibility of Dazzle as ships called into their respective ports and harbours, artists at home and overseas gravitated towards it and some were to be instrumental in the implementation of the camouflage schemes at sea and on land. Many of these artists were part of the traditional maritime painting world, while a select few were associated with the leading modern art movements prior to, during and after the war. The next chapter explores whether Wilkinson himself was inspired by the avant-garde movements of Cubism, Futurism or Vorticism, if it informed his Dazzle painting scheme and how, in turn, his scheme impacted on modern art.

(above) Norman Wilkinson, 'Does not look like any ship you have ever seen', black and white illustration from Henry Newbolt's Submarine and Anti-Submarine *(1918).*

(left) Portrait of Henry Newbolt, etching with drypoint. Private Collection.

Cecil George Charles King (1881–1941),
Dazzled ships at Leith, *1918, watercolour.*
Imperial War Museum (ART 991). Leith
serves as the port of Edinburgh.

CECIL KING
-18-

THE ART AND DESIGN OF DAZZLE IN BRITAIN

Wilkinson's right-hand man at Burlington House was Cecil George Charles King, RNVR (1881–1942). He was a long-standing friend with shared interests in maritime subjects and poster designs which promoted travel by rail and ship. Born in London, King trained at the Westminster School of Art and in Paris, establishing himself as a successful artist and illustrator before and after the war. In private and public he offered moral support to Wilkinson during the prolonged private and public 'camouflage' claims and counter-claims with Professor John Graham Kerr (see Chapter 5). Post-war he continued to support Wilkinson with a letter published in *The Times* on 3 April 1939.

At the outset Wilkinson recorded how the Dazzle designs were distributed through a network of ten men who were not eligible for military service, although their number grew in relation to the workload. They were 'commissioned as Lieutenants RNVR' and allocated to specific ports as 'Dazzle Officers' to supervise the painting of ships. He recollected only the following ports around Britain: London, Southampton, Newcastle, Humber, Glasgow, Liverpool, Bristol, Cardiff and Belfast, although all the major ports were covered. With the exception of London and Liverpool, where two officers were allocated, all the others had one.

In his autobiography Wilkinson reveals very little of the artists themselves, to which ports they were sent or their day-to-day Dazzle work. However, it has been possible to assemble some fascinating information and insights from articles, exhibition reviews, notices and features in newspapers, journals and magazines, as well as Admiralty records, personal reminiscences and biographies.

The Dazzle Officers who either worked at Burlington House and/or as port officers were of diverse ages, backgrounds and expertise. They included the interior and figure painters Leonard Campbell Taylor (1874–1969) and Jan Gordon (1882–1944, real name Godfrey Jervis Gordon); who also painted some landscape scenes and a series of official World War I medical subjects for the Royal Navy afloat and ashore; the landscape artists Charles William Wyllie (1853–1923) and Reginald Guy Kortright (1876–1948); the animal and bird artist Bryan Hook (1856–1925); the hunting and sporting artist Charles Johnson 'Snaffles' Payne (1884–1925); the marine painters Julius Olsson (1864–1942), Frank Henry Mason (1875–1965) and Montague Dawson (1890–1973); the illustrators and poster artists Christopher Clark (1875–1942) and Steven Spurrier (1878–1961); and the Vorticist Edward Alexander Wadsworth (1889–1949).

The Admiralty service records of the RNVR in the National Archives, Kew, provide only basic information, including when the men joined the Dazzle Section. They reveal that at the outset Wilkinson utilized his network of personal connections to secure artists, some of whom were friends, co-students or teachers.

Cecil King joined on 18 August 1917 and was closely followed by one of Wilkinson's art teachers, Julius Olsson, on the 31st of that month. Charles William Wyllie and Montague Dawson were both transferred on 27 August. Wyllie was both a landscape and marine artist who later in life specialized in decorative painting. Dawson's enduring reputation rests on his magnificent clipper-ship paintings and maritime subjects for the *Illustrated London News* and *The Sphere*. His service record indicates that by 20 November 1918 he had been sent to Glasgow to paint naval subjects; and he was present at the surrender of the German fleet at Scapa Flow on 21 November 1918. Angelina Palmer recollects that Wilkinson was not a fan of his work, considering it to be formulaic.

Charles Johnson 'Snaffles' Payne, the immensely popular painter of equine and hunting subjects, joined the Dazzle Section team on 8 September 1917. Some of his wartime experiences were recorded in his autobiography *Snaffles – A Half Century of Memories* (1949). It featured Payne's illustration of a vessel viewed through an enemy periscope, which in his own words 'should demonstrate the method in the apparent madness of the harlequin designs which were bedaubed on ships in convoy in wartime'.

'Snaffles' Payne's passion for camouflage developed over many years and derived from his favourite painting subjects of horse riding and hunting. He wrote: 'For many years the study of Nature's protective coloration in birds and animals has been my very much over-ridden hobby-horse.... I am a champion bore. It must be

obvious to the most casual observer that Mother Nature has taken infinite pains in producing designs which give unobtrusiveness to the hunter and protection to the hunted.'

On 11 September Bryan Hook, the son of the celebrated marine painter James Clarke Hook, had also been 'called up'. On 9 November 1917 Christopher Clark, Jan Gordon and Reginald Guy Kortright were added to the team. The latter had studied with Wilkinson in Paris. Before Christmas 1917 two more artists had been enlisted in the form of Frank Henry Mason (11 December) and Steven Spurrier (19 December). Finally, in the first quarter of 1918 the services were secured of Edward Alexander Wadsworth (27 February) and Leonard Campbell Taylor (22 March).

As this book was nearing completion information on a hitherto unknown Dazzle Officer Oswald Moser

(above) Dazzle Officer Oswald Moser, Courtesy US NHHC.

(opposite) Leonard Campbell Taylor (1874–1969), Herculaneum Dock in Liverpool, 1919 watercolour. Imperial War Museum (ART 2293).

FRANK H. MASON

Edward Yardley, the leading authority on Frank H. Mason, vividly captures the full breadth of the artist's work in his publication *Frank Henry Mason: Marine Painter and Poster Artist* (2015). Seaton Carew-born Mason struggled to make his mark at the naval training establishment HMS *Conway* and abandoned engineering, but their loss was art's gain. Comparable to Wilkinson, he established himself as an accomplished and versatile artist who worked as an author, illustrator, painter, poster designer and printmaker. In addition, he made ship models and was a metal craftsman. Mason produced excellent railway posters, in particular for the London and North Eastern Railway (LNER), although sailing and yachting were his lifelong passion. From the 1890s to 1926 Mason's main residence was in Scarborough (where he had earlier studied art), but from 1927 he settled in London. He was a member of several yacht clubs and was appointed honorary painter to the Royal Thames Yacht Club.

(opposite top) Frank H. Mason (1875–1965) double portrait with Dazzle designs on the walls by Sarony & Co. Courtesy of John White.

(opposite below) Frank Henry Mason, Fabricated Ship Leaving the Tyne, grisaille. Courtesy of the Mitchell Collection.

(below) Frank H. Mason – examples of Dazzle designs from the artist's sketchbook. Courtesy of Edward Yardley.

(bottom) Frank Henry Mason, Protecting Convoy off Scarborough, watercolour. Courtesy of the Mitchell Collection.

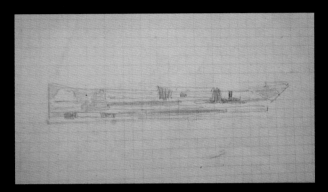

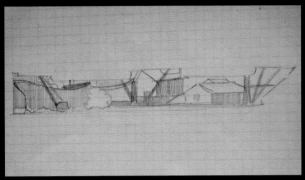

(1874–1953) came to light courtesy of Roy Behrens. This London-born artist, author and illustrator joined the Dazzle Section on 23 November 1917. He trained at the St. John's Wood Art School in London.

On 1 March 1918 Hubert Alington Yockney, RNVR (1888–1969), was transferred to 'The Director of Naval Equipment, Admiralty' and although it is likely he had some involvement with the Dazzle Section it was probably limited because he also worked as a naval war artist. Of his six submissions to the 'Exhibition of Works by Camoufleur Artists' held at the RA in the winter of 1919, one was entitled *Dazzled Ships in Convoy*.

The service record of Philip Gregory Needell, Leading Signalman, RNVR (1886–1974), is surprisingly vague although he exhibited three works at the RA exhibition, including the *HMS 'Almanzora', Ocean Escort, 1917* depicted in Dazzle camouflage.

Although the Admiralty records do not specify the ports to which the artists were sent, it is known from other sources that Mason worked at the Rosyth Dockyard on the Firth of Forth at Rosyth (a port inadvertently omitted on Wilkinson's list) and later Newcastle-upon-Tyne, while Taylor and Wadsworth were based in Liverpool. Guy Kortright also worked there. The subject of works at the aforementioned RA exhibition of 1919 suggests that Bryan Hook worked in Southampton, while Christopher Clark and Steven Spurrier were active in dazzling ships on the Clyde from Glasgow and Greenock.

Wilkinson would have required considerable tact and diplomacy to manage this motley crew of artistic talent in addition to the staff at Burlington House, and it must have tested his supervisory skills to the limit.

Jan Gordon had many interests beyond art. His remarkable life shared with his wife Cora, a fellow artist, author, traveller and musician (they both had a passion for folk music) deserves to be better known today. Gordon also worked as an art critic for *The Observer*. Key aspects of their life, work and travels have been addressed on the websites and blogs of Ken Bryant and Ru Smith (Dr R. D. A. Smith). Gordon's 1918 article 'The Art of Dazzle-Painting' is a eulogy praising Wilkinson's concept, invention and application, although frustratingly it offers no insight into his work as a Dazzle Officer and his relationship with other members of the team, however some remarkable recollections are revealed in extracts from Gordon's private diary covering the period of

6 February to the 27 April 1918 that is now part of Bryant's collection.

On Monday 18 February he wrote, 'I only get at this diary about once a week it seems, other days I lose energy. It seems to require more concentration than I am able to give. The fact is that I do too much during the day. King [Cecil King] today commented on the fact he said he felt done in if he did two designs daily and afterwards only fooled about whereas I have been keeping up an average of 5 to 7 daily now for nearly four months.' Also, in another entry Gordon noted that 'At the office King seized the particular job to design, but as usual got tired of it after he had done the bow and the bridge, and I had to clear it up after him.'

On another occasion Gordon recollected that King 'had designed a paddle steamer, I think very badly – I don't think that either he or Nevinson appreciate the values of black.' Gordon was referring to the war artist C. R. W. Nevinson whose work he had been asked to review and who is addressed in detail later in this chapter.

Gordon designed the Town-class cruiser HMS *Southampton* (1912). He also inspected the vessel in the dockyards of Chatham and Sheerness. During works carried out in the latter dockyard he suggested alterations to the searchlight platform. Also, he recorded that 'the Commander took him on a tour of the ship in the steam pinnace at about 1000 yards. She looked very well tho' not quite as effective as the model.'

In addition to many other vessels Gordon assisted in the creation of Dazzle designs for a 'boat for the Holyhead and Kingston line'. Of the latter he observed that it was 'not a very good design to my mind, too even and too thin'. However, King approved the design. Gordon believed that 'In many ways he is more fussy than Wilkinson and then allows things to pass which I would not.'

Gordon considered that the captains of ships could sometimes pose a problem to the effectiveness of the Dazzle designs. In his own words he produced 'a fairly good design' of HMS *Furious* (1916). This vessel had originally been conceived as a battle cruiser however on 18 March 1917 during her construction she was converted to serve as an aircraft carrier. Gordon went on to explain, 'but as the captain didn't want any white used in it the design isn't as good as it might have been.'

During one trip to the dockyard of Sheerness Gordon was 'fearfully agitated' when he lost his secret Dazzle plans for the oil tanker HMS *Boxleaf* (ex-*Olinda*, 1916).

He remembered last seeing them in his hotel and thought that he might have left them there, or perhaps on a train. Whether or not he reported the incident to HQ is not recorded.

Gordon also recollected that King acquired a 'camera Lucida from a pal in France. With its help and some models I think one could fake up some pretty good sketches of convoy work.'

Bryant notes that Gordon's diary 'ends abruptly, mid paragraph with Jan being posted on a yacht in the Mersey estuary to observe dazzle ships at sea'.

Frank H. Mason was photographed in what is believed to be the studio of the Scarborough-based photographers Sarony & Co perhaps to give a sense of how the Dazzle Section of Burlington House might have appeared [see page 40]. Their studio label is pasted on the back of the photograph. Mason as an RNVR Dazzle officer has been portrayed twice in this novel photograph, both seated and standing, with Dazzle designs hanging on the walls. The image might have been conceived with an official promotional purpose in mind, or for the artist's own personal use. Mason is particularly important in terms of British camouflage

because he was re-engaged to work at the Directorate of Camouflage (Naval Section) located in Leamington Spa during the Second World War.

Twelve artists from the Dazzle Section team contributed artworks to the RA's 'Exhibition of Works by Camoufleur Artists' in 1919. Artists from all the main military camouflage sections – the Camouflage Park, the Camouflage School, the Dazzle Section and the camouflage schools of the Machine Gun Corps and the Tank Corps – were represented in the exhibition. Chaired by Solomon Joseph Solomon (1860–1927), the committee comprised the painters Philip Connard (1875–1958), Henry Mariott Paget (1856–1936), Edward Handley–Read (1870–1935) and Walter Russell (1867–1949), the sculptor Henry Poole (1873–1928), as well as the maritime artists Julius Olsson and Norman Wilkinson.

(above) Christopher Clark, War Paint – S.S. Aquitania, *1918, oil on canvas. Southampton City Council Arts & Heritage.*

The number of artworks displayed by each artist and a selection of their subjects is given below.

CHRISTOPHER CLARK three pictures: *Wartime on the Clyde. 'Dazzle' ships at Greenock*; *'War Paint' – S.S. 'Aquitania,' 1918*; and *Wartime on the Clyde. Discharging Iron ore.*

MONTAGUE DAWSON two pictures: *H.M.S. 'Repulse' chasing. Nov. 17th 1917* and *The Submarine Hunter.*

BRYAN HOOK two pictures: *Southampton Water – September, 1918* and *A Hun ship as Munition Transport passing H.M.S. 'Victory'.*

CECIL KING 15 pictures: including *The Pirates. Transferring German Submarine crews – Harwich, 1918*; *The Mole extension and the 'Brussels,' Zeebrugge*; *Italian Cruiser 'Coatit' off Gibraltar'*; and *First dazzle design of H.M.T. 'Briton'.*

FRANK HENRY MASON three pictures: *War Time Colour. River Tyne. Conversion of H.M.S. 'Furious' into an Aeroplane Carrier. Tyne auxiliary Patrol Base and Neutral shipping*; *'Lining Off' War Nizam and H.M.S. 'Dauntless'*; and *'Conjecture'.*

PHILIP GREGORY NEEDELL three pictures: *H.M.S. 'Almanzora' Ocean Escort, 1917*; *The Convoy; November 11th, 1918. H.M.S. 'Almanzora' at Sierra Leone*; and *'Hostilities to be suspended forthwith'.*

JULIUS OLSSON one picture: *Off Dover.*

STEVEN SPURRIER six pictures, including: *Repairs in Dry Dock*; *Worn by the Weather*; *A Repaint*; and *At Rothesay Dock.*

EDWARD WADSWORTH four pictures, all woodcuts: *Turret Ship in Dry Dock*; *S.S. 'Jerseymoor'*; *Dry-docked for scaling and painting*; and *Liverpool Shipping – 1918.*

NORMAN WILKINSON two pictures: *Convoy* and *You are standing into a Minefield*. Wilkinson's primary duties in heading up the Dazzle Section clearly impacted on the amount of free time he had to paint pictures for exhibitions.

CHARLES WILLIAM WYLLIE two pictures: *British Aeroplane in Storm attacking German Troops on the march* and *Sea-plane returning to Base*. The latter was lent by *The Sphere* magazine.

HUBERT ALINGTON YOCKNEY six pictures, including: *British Monitors bombarding Zeebrugge, 1915, Dover Patrol – Monitors and light forces attacked by enemy aircraft off the Belgian Coast, 1916*; *'Drifter Patrol' by night Dazzled Ships in Convoy* and *Surrendered German Warships at Scapa Flow.*

Edward Wadsworth stands out among the Dazzle Officers as the only avant-garde artist. Jan Gordon recorded in his diary when he first caught sight of him at Burlington House on Tuesday 5th March 1918. Gordon described him as, '...long, lean, side whiskered looking rather like a print from Dickens period of dandyism.' He also stated that 'I shall now know if he is really a great artist. If his designs are better than mine I shall in future respect his work for his ideas are founded on design (so he says or so they say for him)...'

Prior to the outbreak of war Wadsworth was an active member of the Vorticists, a radical British art group. Vorticism was an Anglo-American art movement established in London in 1914 and led by Percy Wyndham Lewis (1882–1957). The group, in general terms, created art to express the dynamism of the modern world. It was inspired by and largely drew upon the artistic techniques of and subjects from the French and Italian modern art movements of Cubism (established *c.*1907) and Futurism (established in 1909), and to a lesser extent the Expressionism that overlaps with these two. Of the former, the founders and best-known exponents were George Braque and Pablo Picasso; and the latter led by Filippo Marinetti had many

(opposite) Edward Wadsworth (1889–1949), Liverpool Shipping – 1918. Woodcut on Japan paper. The powerful visual impact of Wadsworth's dry dock shipping scene relates to the artist's service as a Dazzle Officer in Liverpool during World War I. He produced a series of related Dazzle artworks that include the cover of this publication entitled Camouflaged Ship in Dry Dock – 1918 which in 1923 was adapted for a poster and catalogue cover of an exhibition of British prints in Zurich. Four years later the artist burnt all the original wood blocks from which his prints were taken declaring that 'they're finished and done with'.

Private Collection/© Estate of Edward Wadsworth. All Rights Reserved. DACS 2016. Photo © The Fine Art Society London/ Bridgeman Images.

followers including Giacomo Balla, Umberto Boccioni, Carlo Carrà and Gino Severini.

The Cubists dispensed with the illusion of depth on a picture's surface. In came the fragmentation and flattening out of objects and figures that could be seen from several viewpoints simultaneously. The French art dealer René Gimpel's experience, recollected in *Diary of an Art Dealer* (John Rosenberg, tr. 1966), of seeing one Dazzled ship brought to mind 'an enormous Cubist painting with great sheets of ultramarine blue, black and green, sometimes parallel but more often with sharp corners cleaving into one another, and, although you don't quite make it out, you can divine a reason, a plan – a guiding principle'.

The Futurists wanted to celebrate cars, youth and violence. They favoured the illusion of rapid movement and speed, and were preoccupied with machine-age subjects and urban scenes.

Vorticism adapted and reinterpreted the movements' ideologies and visual languages. Above all it embraced the industrial age, visualizing it with angular and machine-like forms. Although there were doctrinal differences, and Lewis despised the Futurists, Vorticism had more commonality with the Futurism movement.

In 1915 the Vorticists held their first and last London exhibition. Two years later there was a solo show at the Penguin Club in New York. Two editions of the Vorticist magazine *BLAST* appeared in June 1914 and July 1915, which contained 'blasting' manifestos by Lewis. Other artists associated with the group included Lawrence Atkinson, Jessica Dismorr, Frederick Etchells, Cuthbert Hamilton, William Roberts, Helen Saunders and Dorothy Shakespear; the sculptors Sir Jacob Epstein and Henri Gaudier-Brzeska; the photographer Alvin Langdon Coburn, who created Vortographs, and graphic designer El Lissitzky, whose skills gave *BLAST* its distinctive appearance. David Bomberg, although not officially part of the group, also executed work in a similar style. One of his best-known works is *The Mud Bath* (1914), which is part of the primary collections on public display in Tate Britain.

Wilkinson was a traditional maritime artist working in a style that has been described by the art historian Jonathan Black as 'quasi-Impressionist'. By the mid-1910s Impressionism was a conservative rather than a cutting-edge art movement. Wilkinson surrounded himself with fellow artists, many of whom were antagonistic to avant-garde art. David Cuppleditch, in his history of *The London Sketch Club* (1994), noted that Picasso was the artist who annoyed its members more than any other. Jan Gordon, a London Sketch Club member, collaborated with the cartoonist Henry Mayo Bateman to produce their publication *Art Ain't All Paint* (1944). On its cover is a ludicrous-looking artist at his easel, portrayed in Cubist style and painting a Cubist portrait. However, it would be dangerous to judge the book by its cover. Gordon had studied in Paris and was in fact an admirer of Picasso and modern art movements. In *Modern French Painters*, published in 1923, he wrote a carefully considered essay on Cubism. A presentation copy of this publication is in the collection of Bryant and is inscribed to his life-long friend and fellow Dazzle Officer Stephen Spurrier with the words 'To my old pal Spurrier in memory of the purest art we ever touched. Dazzle.'

(above) Cover of BLAST *(1915).*

(opposite) Norman Wilkinson, 'Was repainted in...futurist colours'. Portrait of HMS Canopus *from Henry Newbolt's* Tales of the Great War *(1916).*

Jonathan Black's essay '"A few broad stripes":
Perception, deception and the "Dazzle ship" phenomenon
of the First World War' in *Contested Objects: Material
memories of the Great War* (2014) states that 'as far as can
be ascertained...Wilkinson was not familiar with pre-war
avant-garde geometrical abstraction' – that is, Cubism,
Futurism, Vorticism and Orphism, an offshoot of Cubism
that focused on pure abstraction and vivid colours. Black
may well be right, but the following small-scale piece
of visual evidence raises some intriguing questions in
terms of the time frame of the development of Dazzle
painting in relation to modern art movements as well as
Wilkinson's familiarity with earlier 'camouflage' schemes.

Throughout his career Wilkinson illustrated many
publications. They included Henry Newbolt's *Tales of
the Great War* (1916), embellished with 'seven coloured
plates and thirty-two illustrations in black and white
by Norman Wilkinson and Christopher Clark'. This is
the same Clark who served as a Dazzle Officer. One of
Wilkinson's black-and-white illustrations features in
the chapter 'The Story of Two Admirals' and depicts
HMS *Canopus* covered in what appears to be a Dazzle
design. The illustration is initialled 'NW', dated 1916
and captioned 'Was repainted in...futurist colours'. Even
in the medium of black and white you can see the bold
geometric designs on the hull, funnels and upper parts
of the ship. They do not appear to be an attempt to
conceal the ship but rather to break up her outlines in
accordance with Dazzle painting.

What does the background and service history of
HMS *Canopus* reveal of her 'camouflage' schemes? The
ship was built at Portsmouth Dockyard and launched
in 1879. She was the lead ship of the *Canopus* class with
a complement of 750 and a speed of 18 knots. The ship
featured in Newbolt's publication in relation to her war
service in the Falklands. Initially, she was active in the
search for Admiral Maximilian von Spee's German East
Asia Squadron; however, she was not fast enough to
follow Rear Admiral Christopher Cradock's armoured
cruisers and therefore missed the Battle of Coronel on 1
November 1914. However, the ship did fire the opening
shots of the Battle of the Falklands, this time led by Vice
Admiral Frederick Charles Doveton Sturdee. On the
morning of 8 December 1914 Admiral von Spee sent the
Gneisenau and the *Nürnberg* on a skirmishing mission.
They were sighted off Port Stanley, where Sturdee's ships
lay at anchor. The *Canopus* opened fire and the German

'Was repainted in . . . futurist colours.'

ships retreated to rejoin their squadron. By the end of the
day all but one of the German ships had been sunk and
von Spee went down with the *Scharnhorst*.

Newbolt recounted:

*Port Stanley was reoccupied and fortified in the most
spirited fashion by the inhabitants, and the officers
and men of the Canopus. The smaller guns of the
battleship were landed and mounted in good positions
ashore; the good old ship herself was evidently not fast
enough or strong enough to fight the whole German
Squadron at sea, so it was decided to turn her into a
fort. She was taken into the inner harbour and then
anchored fast on a mud-bank, under the narrow strip
of land which divides the harbour from the sea. This
strip or ridge was high enough to give her a
good parapet to fire over; and to make her a still
more difficult target for the enemy's guns, she was
repainted in what Mr. William Buchan describes as
'futurist colours'. This gave her all the chance her men
could expect...*

Newbolt does not reveal William Buchan's role
during the action, but his expression 'futurist colours' is
fascinating. Did Buchan intend to associate the painted
design on the ship with the art movement of Futurism,

or to imply – as defined in the *Oxford Advanced Learners Dictionary* – that what he saw was 'extremely modern and unusual in appearance, as if belonging to a future time'? Given the lower case 'f' of futurist it is more likely to be the latter, although prior to the Gallipoli campaign the words Futurism and Futurist referring to the art movement, and a member of it, had entered the British public domain.

What can be deduced from Wilkinson's illustration of HMS *Canopus* dated 1916 is that he was familiar with a camouflage scheme that had similarities to his own later invention. In this instance the ship had been painted according to Professor Kerr's 'parti-colouring' scheme. Kerr's scheme had been distributed to the Fleet in a confidential General Order on 10 November 1914. Whether or not Wilkinson was aware of Kerr's scheme is addressed in Chapter 5, because this was identified as the key issue by the Royal Commission on Awards to Inventors (RCAI) in determining whether or not Wilkinson should be awarded the Dazzle painting 'prize'.

The *Canopus* was later transferred to the Mediterranean, for the Dardanelles Campaign, where she would once again be painted with 'dazzle patterns'. The British-born soldier Harry Askin recollected his first encounter with the *Canopus* and it was later published in Jean Baker's *A Marine at Gallipoli on The Western Front: First In, Last Out – The Diary of Harry Askin* (2015). After a brief stop-over at Moudros in the middle of April 1915 Askin arrived at the picturesque island of Skyros where he saw the ship in 'fine natural harbour'. He wrote: 'The old battleship was in, also a troopship. *Canopus* did look a pot mess; her crew were painting dazzle patterns on her.'

This certainly proves that the word 'dazzle' was being used to describe painted camouflage on ships as early as April 1915, prior to Wilkinson's invention of Dazzle painting in 1917. The old battleship's camouflage is likely to have played a part in the ship surviving the war and she was decommissioned in April 1919.

Edward Wadsworth was certainly inspired by his work as a Dazzle Officer to produce some of the most accomplished, visually arresting and memorable small scale black and white woodcuts, some lithographs and a vast oil painting of Dazzle-painted ships during and immediately after the war. They were inextricably linked to his active war service. The woodcut *Camouflaged ship in dry dock – 1918* features on the cover of this book.

Edward Alexander Wadsworth was born in Cleckheaton in West Yorkshire, the son of a prominent worsted-spinning businessman. Schooling at Ghyll Royd at Ilkley and Fettes College in Edinburgh was followed by the study of machine draughtsmanship in Munich (1906–1907) with an eye to following in the family business. At this time he also studied at the popular Heinrich Knirr painting school, which prompted a change of career.

After returning to Yorkshire, he attended the Bradford School of Art before securing a scholarship to the Slade School of Fine Art, where his contemporaries included Adrian Allinson, David Bomberg, Mark Gertler, Christopher Richard Wynne Nevinson and Stanley Spencer. Nevinson (1889–1946) was closely allied with Vorticism, although he fell out with Lewis over his membership of the Futurists. He produced many art works which combined formal elements of Cubism and Futurism, in terms of fragmentation of form and the illusion of rapid movement. These works include *The Arrival* (c.1913) and *Returning to the Trenches* (1916) the latter inspired by active service on the Western Front. The former at first sight produces the same effects desired by Wilkinson's Dazzle painting scheme.

I n 1913 Wadsworth contributed Cubist landscapes to Roger Fry's second *Post-Impressionist Exhibition, British, French and Russian Artists* at the Grafton Galleries in London, but changed artistic direction after befriending the polemicist Wyndham Lewis, a friendship that lasted a lifetime. Both artists were invited by Fry to produce work for the Omega Workshops alongside Frederick Etchells and Cuthbert Hamilton, although their residence there was short-lived, lasting from July to October 1913. During the period from October of that year to July 1914, when Wadsworth settled in London, he contributed to a diverse range of exhibitions, including: the Cubist Room Section of an exhibition by the *Camden Town Group and Others* at the Brighton Public Art Galleries; *The First Exhibition of Works by Members of the London Group* at the Goupil Gallery, London; he joined Lewis' Rebel Art Centre located in Great Ormond Street; and submitted works to *Twentieth Century Art,*

(opposite) Christopher Richard Wynne Nevinson (1889-1946) Returning to the Trenches, *woodcut from* BLAST *(1915).*

a Review of Modern Movements held at the Whitechapel Art Gallery, as well as the London Salon of Allied Artists' Association at Holland Park Hall, London.

On 20 June 1914 Wadsworth had signed the Vorticist group's manifesto. It was to be a short-lived movement. The worldwide devastation caused by man and machine during the First World War overpowered and overshadowed the Vorticists' artistic aspirations to visually capture the energy and dynamism of the industrial machine age.

In the post-war era Wadsworth moved away from the avant-garde and abstraction towards a more realistic style, producing some paintings influenced by Surrealism. In 1921 he became a member of the New English Art Club and in 1933 joined Unit One, the short-lived British group formed by Paul Nash to promote modern art, architecture and design, and in the following year he contributed to their only exhibition. Cunard commissioned two enormous maritime paintings from

him to adorn the transatlantic liner RMS *Queen Mary* that sailed on her maiden voyage to New York in 1936.

Some of Wadsworth's friends felt that he had betrayed his artistic and rebellious principles by becoming an Associate Member of the RA in 1943. By this time it had become an archly conservative organization. In 1944 Alfred Munnings, the celebrated equine artist, took over as president and was an outspoken critic of past and present avant-garde art. During a radio broadcast on the BBC in 1949 Munnings claimed that the work of Cézanne, Matisse and Picasso had corrupted art.

From early June 1916 Wadsworth was active in the eastern Mediterranean, working as an intelligence officer examining and interpreting aerial reconnaissance photographs taken by the Royal Naval Air Service. He was invalided home a year later on medical grounds and eventually 'passed fit for shore service' before being formally transferred to the Dazzle Section on 27 February 1918.

'THE ARRIVAL'

Nevinson combined elements of Cubism and Futurism to brilliant effect in his maritime masterpiece *The Arrival*. Painted around 1913 the picture, according to Tate Britain specialists, baffled one reviewer when it was first publicly displayed. He commented: 'It resembles a Channel steamer after a violent collision with a pier. You detect funnels, smoke, gangplanks, distant hotels, numbers, posters all thrown into the melting-pot, so to speak.' He went on to explain that Mr. Nevinson acted as interpreter, explaining that it represented a state of simultaneous mind'. In other words he wanted to capture 'the multitude of views and movements happening at a single moment'.

At first sight *The Arrival* brings to mind the experience of looking at a scene or view through a shattered glass window. The jarring lines and stark colour contrasts make it difficult at first to make out the overall outline and size of the ocean liner, although with careful scrutiny you can reassemble the pieces into an intelligible picture. The technique is different to that applied to a Dazzled ship, although the immediate confusion confronting the viewer mirrors the intention of Wilkinson's scheme.

Uppingham-educated Nevinson had been advised by Henry Tonks, Professor of Drawing at the Slade, to abandon his ambition to become a painter. Fortunately, he did not concur. In addition to his avant-garde style, Nevinson later adopted a gritty realism into his subjects of the war-torn landscape of northern France. His depictions of the wounded and dead on the barren battlefields of the Western Front in predominately earthy colours pack a powerful emotional punch. They rank very highly among the finest of all the war art of the period.

(above) Christopher Richard Wynne Nevinson (1889–1946), The Arrival (circa 1913), oil on canvas. © Tate London 2016 .

(opposite) SS Zealandia (1910). Photograph from the Green Collection. State of Victoria Library.

The art historian Richard Cork considers that Wilkinson 'might have been influenced on a subliminal level by the work of the avant-garde, and his decision to involve Wadsworth surely implies an awareness on Wilkinson's part of Vorticist work'. However, it can also be convincingly argued that on a purely practical level Wilkinson simply responded quickly to the fact that he had at his disposal a professional artist, of non-combatant age, with some seafaring experience who was willing and able to work.

In terms of his Dazzle painting work, Wadsworth worked with Leonard Campbell Taylor in Liverpool. Barbara Wadsworth, the daughter of the artist, recollects in the biography of her father, *Edward Wadsworth – A Painter's Life* (1989), that in April he worked initially in Bristol but by July 1918 he was relocated to Liverpool and headquartered at the Royal Liver Building'. Taylor was an older artist with little interest in modern art. He had trained at the the the St. John's Wood Art School and the Royal Academy Schools, and was known for his carefully crafted interior scenes and portraits executed in a quasi-Impressionist style. He was elected RA in 1931.

From Wadsworth's personal photographic record of the ships he worked on it is known that they ranged from the modest to majestic. They included the single-funnel cargo and passenger carrier SS *Zealandia* (1910), built for Huddart, Parker & Co of Melbourne, that served as a troopship in both world wars; several ocean liners, including the Allan Line's SS *Alsatian* (1912), later owned by Canadian Pacific and renamed the *Empress of France* in 1919; also the two four-funnel Cunarders RMS *Mauretania* (1906) and RMS *Aquitania* (1914), both of which survived the war.

Jonathan Black is confident that although most of the Dazzle painting designs originated in London, Wilkinson 'always gave his port officers latitude to extemporize'. On the other hand, the cultural historian Robert Hewison, in his paper 'Cutting and Dazzling – Edward Wadsworth, Vorticism and Woodcuts', which was presented at the Vorticist International Symposium on 29 January 2011, argues that Wadsworth acted solely in a supervisory capacity. Barbara Wadsworth also pondered on the degree of his involvement with the designs. She wrote: 'In alluding to this period in his life he referred to it as "when I was working on Camouflage ships", and this is, admittedly, ambiguous; yet he never gave the impression that he did not design, and the several photographs he kept, with their jagged stripes and curved forms, would seem to indicate a more personal interest.'

The men painting the ships had, without question, to be carefully monitored. 'Snaffles' Payne, as reported by the military historian Guy Hartcup, was adamant that 'the execution of the design by gangs of workmen had to be strictly supervised, otherwise lifeboats and Carley floats' would be overlooked. And that 'ineffective and dangerous designs were all traced to the dazzle being painted by people who did not grasp the principle of the scheme'. Hartcup also pointed out an additional challenge that 'some of the captains did not care for "jazz" designs because they made the ships look slovenly'.

The artists were under orders, as commissioned officers, to supervise the Dazzle-painted ships from plans created at and issued by Burlington House however new evidence from Jan Gordon's diary reveals that the Officers were on occasions given the freedom to create their own designs. As time was of the essence to get each ship ready for active service – and as the vessels required repainting every four to six months – it made sense to empower the Dazzle Officers allocated to the ports when necessary to deviate from the official plans and contribute something of their own making, although Wilkinson was insistent that only the official authorized colours should be used as per the plans issued from Burlington House.

Cork's admiration for Wadsworth's wartime work in fine art form is now widespread. He states 'the sight of the mighty vessels receiving their patterns in dry-dock provided Wadsworth with ready-made subjects for his own art'. He also remarks: 'During 1918 he found time to produce an outstanding series of woodcuts each one of which revelled in the optical bite of the bands surging their way across the ship's surface.'

John Duncan Fergusson (1874–1961), Dockyard, Portsmouth, *1918, oil on canvas. Imperial War Museum (ART 5728). Courtesy of the Fergusson Gallery, Perth and Kinross Council. Fergusson is best known as a Scottish Colourist. He was not part of Wilkinson's Dazzle team, although he painted some striking Dazzle subjects.*

Wadsworth exhibited drawings and woodcuts at the Adelphi Gallery, London, in March 1919, and in 'A Note' published in the exhibition catalogue by fellow Vorticist Frederick Etchells, he audaciously claimed that 'dazzle-camouflage [another term for Dazzle painting] would probably never have developed as it did had it not been for the experiments in abstract design made by a few modern artists during the years immediately prior to 1914'.

There is no substantial evidence to support this self-interested claim. What can be confidently stated is that it was the combination of Wadsworth's active participation as a Vorticist in tandem with his work as a Dazzle Officer that resulted in the brilliant Dazzle designs in printed and painted fine art formats.

Etchells was not the only artist to make such a bold claim. Earlier, Gertrude Stein recollected an incident in Paris that later featured in her publication *Picasso* (1938). She wrote 'at the beginning of the war being with Picasso on the Boulevard Raspail when the first camouflaged truck passed. It was at night, we had heard of camouflage but we had not seen it and then cried out, yes it was we who made it – that is cubism'.

In France there had been a rapid response to establish an official camouflage department, albeit one that focused primarily on land-based subjects. On 12 February 1915 General Joseph Joffre, Commander-in-Chief of the French forces on the Western Front, formed the Section de Camouflage at Amiens. Several of the *camoufleurs* were professional artists that had an empathy with the Cubist work of Braque and Picasso.

Lucien-Victor Guirand de Scévola (1871–1950) was an artistic pioneer of camouflage. By the end of 1915 he was appointed commander of the Section de Camouflage. Ordinarily, de Scévola practised as a high-society portraitist working in pastels in a style influenced by Symbolism, although during the war he embraced the Cubist idiom for his camouflage work. In *Dazzled and Deceived – Mimicry and Camouflage* (2009), Peter Forbes noted de Scévola's statement: 'In order to deform totally the aspect of an object, I had to employ the means that cubists use to represent it.'

From July 1915 de Scévola had secured the services of another *camoufleur* André Mare (1885–1932), the artist, author, designer and practitioner of Cubism. Several of his sketchbooks have survived and among the notable Cubist works is *Le canon de 280 camouflé*. They are in the collection of the Historial de la Grande Guerre,

Château de Péronne. De Scévola's team later expanded to include the artists Charles Camoin, Charles Dufresne, André Dunoyer de Segonzac and Jacques Villon.

Mare also worked for the Italian and British armies; and in recognition of his valuable war service, on 10 August 1916 he was awarded the Military Cross by King George V. Perhaps it is this connection that has led some to speculate that Wilkinson was aware of Cubism. Among their number is Jonathan Black, who suggests that he 'may have been aware of the qualified Cubist schemes produced for the French army by *camoufleurs*'.

Returning to the Dazzle work of Wadsworth, Cork also believes that it was the culmination of the artist's long-standing preoccupation with stripes that first emerged before the war and is evident in the 'boldly patterned shawl' of the striking *Portrait of Mrs Violet Wallis* (current whereabouts unknown); and that this enduring interest could be linked to the Vorticist manifesto. In the second edition of *BLAST*, published in 1915, Lewis asserted that 'the striped awnings of Cafes and shops, the stripes of bathing tents, the stripes of bathing-machines, of toy trumpets, of dresses, are marshalled into a dense essence of the scene'.

In early October 1919 Wadsworth exhibited four woodcuts at the RA's 'Exhibition of Works by Camoufleur Artists'. A notice appeared in *The Times* on 7 October 1919 subheaded 'War Secrets Revealed'. The exhibition occupied three galleries at Burlington House and it included 'the naval dazzle-painting section'. The reviewer observed: 'The baffling effects of dazzle-painting are well shown in a number of paintings and drawings, conspicuous among which is Christopher Clark's picture of the *Aquitania* completely broken up with stripes and zig-zags and other strange markings.' Clark's large oil painting, measuring 37in by 65in (95cm by 165cm), is now in the collection of the Southampton City Museums.

Wadsworth's woodcuts were also on display. *The Evening Standard* in November 1919 reported: '...the "dazzle" section illustrates amusingly an inversion of the principles of Post-Impressionism – how to destroy form instead of emphasising it – and the woodcuts of ships by Mr Edward Wadsworth, are by far the best things artistically in the exhibition.'

Several of these woodcuts were produced by Wadsworth during his time as a port-based Dazzle Officer. Befitting his position, all the vessels were depicted in port with some in dry-dock. Four of them

– *Turret Ship in Dry Dock*, *Dry-docked for scaling and painting*, *Dazzle Ship in Dry-dock* and *Dock Scene* – capture the vibrancy and visual confusion caused by the curvilinear lines and striped lines; while a fifth, called *Minesweepers in Port*, features stark and diagonal lines and saw-tooth patterns found in other Dazzle designs.

An examination of Wadsworth's earlier woodcut of *Newcastle*, first published in the inaugural edition of *BLAST* in 1914, reveals several similarities in terms of content and style to his series of 1918. The curvilinear and zig-zag lines and saw-tooth patterns typical of Dazzle can be seen in this picture. However, Wadsworth never claimed that Dazzle painting derived from Vorticism.

From his woodcut *Liverpool Shipping – 1918* [see page 45], measuring overall less than 30.38 cm (1 foot), Wadsworth developed the vast oil painting entitled *Dazzle-ships in Dry Dock at Liverpool – 1919* of more than 289.56 cm (9 $\frac{1}{2}$ feet) in height. Now on display in the National Gallery of Canada, the painting had

been commissioned by the Anglo-Canadian press baron Max Aitken, Lord Beaverbrook, for the Canadian War Memorial that he established in 1916. Later, in 1936, it was transformed into a poster for the Imperial War Museum to encourage visitors to visit the new museum that had moved from South Kensington to Lambeth Road, close to Waterloo station, and where it remains today.

Beyond Burlington House there were also many British artists who became fascinated with Dazzle-painted ships, and not surprisingly many of them already had a preference for marine painting and maritime subjects. Among the noteworthy are Geoffrey Allfree [pages 88–89], Muirhead Bone, Charles Bryant, Thomas Derrick, Francis Dodd, Sholto J. Douglas, John Duncan Fergusson [page 52], John Lavery, Donald Maxwell, Charles Pears [pages 4–5, 11, 81], Noel Sampson, Kenneth Denton Shoesmith[page 87], Philip Wilson Steer and John Wheatley.

In terms of numbers, quality and commitment to the subject of Dazzle painting in their art during the war, the artist John Everett stands out from rest. Gwen Yarker a former curator of the National Maritime Museum (NMM), writes that Herbert Barnard John Everett (1876–1949):

> ...occupies a unique position in the canon of marine painting. At his death, almost his entire marine output of 2,752 oils, prints and drawings produced over a 50-year period, came to the NMM. His comprehensive legacy affords a rare opportunity to examine a lifetime's artistic response to the sea, based on close observation and personal experience.

Everett undertook extensive sea voyages, sometimes as a working member of the crew. As a man of private means, he made no serious attempt to earn a living from his art and was freed from the academic artistic demands of his professional contemporaries. His denial of the path taken by his artistic equals, combined with an avowed fear of publicity has meant that his considerable output has been largely overlooked by scholars of early 20th-century English painting.

Dorchester-born Everett, like Wilkinson, studied with Louis Grier and Julius Olsson in St. Ives, Cornwall. He also attended the Slade School of Fine Art, where his contemporaries included the British Impressionist painter Philip Wilson Steer, Augustus and Gwen John

PAINTINGS & DRAWINGS
OF THE
CAMOUFLAGE
OF SHIPS
BY
JOHN EVERETT
AT THE
GOUPIL GALLERY
5 REGENT ST. S.W.1
ADMISSION 1s.3d. INCLUDING TAX
DAILY 10 to 5   SATURDAYS 10 to 1

and Percy Wyndham Lewis; and briefly at the Académie Julian in Paris. The British Impressionist artist Laura Knight described Everett in her memoirs, *Oil Paint and Grease Paint* (1936), as being a 'typical Englishman; his pale blue eyes, fair skin, rough tweeds and thick boots singled him out astonishingly as he went his own way'.

In the spring of 1918 Everett was commissioned by the Ministry of Information to create drawings and paintings of the London docks, the river and mouth of the Thames, some of which were later exhibited in the USA. In many of them Everett explored the visual effects of Wilkinson's 'camouflage'. For example, in *Convoy* (1918) [pages 72–73] he created a curvilinear sea in response to the geometric patterns on the Dazzled ships.

In his unpublished memoirs, *Wicked Devils, Wicked Devils* (1945), Everett wrote: 'The Ministry of Information went out of existence in Nov. 11th 1918. I could have sold all the works I did in the docks during the war. After the war everybody was so fed up, they wouldn't look at any war thing. In Nov. I had a show of 50 things at the Goupil Gallery in Lower Regent Street. I only sold one, to H.G. Wells'. A copy of the exhibition poster, featuring a stylized Dazzled steamship, promoting Everett's *Paintings & Drawings of the Camouflage of Ships* has survived and can be seen in the Imperial War Museum. The admission charge of '1s.3d including tax' indicated on the poster would also have deterred some visitors.

(opposite) Herbert Barnard John Everett (1876–1949), poster advertising his exhibition at the Goupil Gallery. Imperial War Museum (PST 8553).

(above) H. B. J.Everett, Cunarder converting into an armed merchantmen, *1918, oil on canvas. National Maritime Museum. Greenwich, London.*

DAZZLE IN THE USA

E arly in 1918 Admiral William Sowden Sims, the commander of the United States Navy's forces in Europe, visited London to investigate what could be done in terms of the protection of American merchant vessels. Shortly afterwards Wilkinson received a formal request from the United States Navy (USN) Department to travel to Washington, D.C., to advise them on his Dazzle painting scheme. It was also described as 'baffle painting'; however, contrary to popular opinion, it was only occasionally referred to as 'Razzle Dazzle'.

Wilkinson insisted that he take his wife as a secretary. Rather than it being a personal indulgence, she had work experience in the Dazzle Section at Burlington House where, as Miss Mackenzie, they had first met and she was therefore an asset.

The Wilkinsons arrived in New York on the ocean liner USS *Leviathan*, originally the *Vaterland*, probably in early February although the precise date is not known. The ship had been built by Blohm and Voss for the Hamburg-America Line's transatlantic route and seized by the United States Shipping Board (USSB) after the declaration of war on Germany on 6 April 1917. She was converted into a troopship and later Dazzled. After the Wilkinsons' arrival they took the train to the capital city where they were met by the Assistant Secretary of the Navy (ASN) Franklin D. Roosevelt, who later became President of the United States.

Wilkinson recollected that Roosevelt told him,

(above) Portrait of Admiral William Sowden Sims. Library of Congress.

(opposite) Arthur Lismer (1885–1969), RMS *Olympic in dazzle paint at Halifax, Nova Scotia, oil on canvas. Courtesy Canadian Museum of History.*

'we have brought you here because we understand that the system of ship camouflage which you have originated is the most successful available'. Roosevelt wanted to replicate the Dazzle Section of Burlington House in Washington, D.C., so that designs could be distributed to key ports across the United States. Roosevelt continued: 'We have no department of camouflage here. We want to find a house with a suitable room to put up your temporary theatre and other rooms for offices.'

In order to develop the scheme Wilkinson had 'to make a tour of all the major United States dockyards, to deliver a lecture at each of them on my system, its objects, how it worked and was to be applied'. All located on the northeastern seaboard, the ports were Boston, New York, Philadelphia, Washington, D.C., and Norfolk, Virginia, the furthest south.

Wilkinson does not address in any detail the artists he encountered while working on the US scheme. However, information has been gleaned from some of the serving American artists, especially Everett Longley Warner who was tasked to escort Wilkinson during his work in the USA; and through the remarkable wide-ranging research and publications on camouflage by Roy R. Behrens, Professor of Art at the University of Northern Iowa. Behrens' Camoupedia is now the most important online resource for anyone interested in the subject of camouflage – it is an extension of his *Camoupedia: A Compendium of Research on Art, Architecture and Camouflage* first published in April 2009. Through this resource Behrens has facilitated not only the assemblage of material on naval camouflage but also provided new insights into the organizational structure of the official

camouflage departments in the USA.

In February 1918 the Impressionist painter and printmaker Everett Longley Warner had been commissioned as a lieutenant in the US Naval Reserves. Warner was appointed the director of the Design subdivision of the newly established American Camouflage Section. Located in Washington, D.C., the subdivision was comprised mostly of artistic people, who included: the marine painter Frederick Judd Waugh (1861–1940) and the sculptor John Gregory (1879–1958); the artists Kenneth Stevens MacIntire (1891–1979), Manley Kercheval Nash (1882–1947) and Gordon Stevenson (1892–1982); the architect Raymond J. Richardson and the advertising artist M. O'Connell.

A second subdivision, staffed mostly by scientists, focused on camouflage research and was based at the Eastman Kodak Company in Rochester, New York. It was directed by Lieutenant Loyd A. Jones (1884–1954) whose academic training and specialisms included

USS Leviathan *originally named* Vaterland. *Courtesy US NHHC.*

(opposite) Harold van Buskirk (1894–1980) standing in the background examining Dazzle ship models. Courtesy Roy R. Behrens (PD).

(right) A photograph of US Navy camouflage artists during World War I. It was initially published on the title page of a magazine article called "Fooling the Iron Fish: The Inside Story of Marine Camouflage" in Everybody's Magazine (November 1919), pp. 102–109 written by Everett Longley Warner. He was the officer in charge of the design subsection in Washington DC of the Navy's Camouflage Section. He is seated on the far left, while (from left to right) the other camoufleurs include Frederick Judd Waugh (1861–1940), John Gregory (1879–1958), Gordon Stevenson (1892–1982), Manley Kercheval Nash (1882–1947) (in the right foreground), and M. O'Connell. Courtesy Roy R. Behrens (PD).

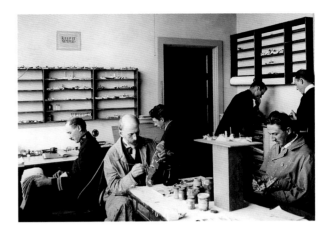

(far left) Everett Longly Warner (1877–1963). Warner family.

(left) Painted ship models. Gordon Stevenson is standing in the centre background. The other artists include (left to right) sculptor John Gregory, marine painter Frederick Waugh, and theatrical scene painter Manley K. Nash. Courtesy Roy R. Behrens (PD).

physics and optics. A compromise was reached between the competitive artists and scientists in terms of who should take overall control of the two subdivisions and this appointment was given to the architect and fencing champion Lieutenant Harold Van Buskirk (1894–1980).

A photograph of the Model Painting Room (c.1918) was published in the November 1919 issue of *Everybody's Magazine* to accompany an article written by Warner entitled 'Fooling the Iron Fish: The Inside Story of Marine Camouflage'. Warner is seated on the far left, while from left to right the workers include Waugh, Gregory, Stevenson, Nash (in the foreground) and O'Connell. Another photograph of a different room dated 12 July 1918 depicts the camoufleurs painting ship models. From left to right can be seen Gregory, Waugh and Nash, with Stevenson standing. A third photograph shows Van Buskirk with Raymond J. Richardson, who was in charge of the drafting room; a fourth probably depicts Richardson in the ship model store; while a

fifth photograph shows a group of camoufleurs in the drafting room of the Design subsection in 1918. All these photographs have been published on Camoupedia.

The key questions about what colors were used on First World War American camouflaged ships, and in what combination, have been asked and posted by Behrens, who has answered them by stating, 'It seems we can never be certain, since apparently no color photographs were made of them'. Although he also noted that some hand-painted models exist.

Compared to Wilkinson, Lieutenant Loyd A. Jones had access to greater resources, especially in relation to testing space. To test the Dazzle designs he set up a sophisticated theatre that featured an observation tank, an artificial sun and a movable sky viewable through a submarine periscope. He also had the outdoor option to test the Dazzle patterns on both miniature models and painted cut-out silhouettes on the shore of Lake Ontario. Behrens has divided the process of painting the ships

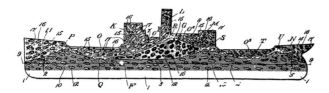

From top: various illustrations related to US Dazzle. Below: William Andrew Mackay (1876–1939). Images courtesy Camoupedia.

into 'six steps': Devising a Distortion Plan, Building & Painting a Model, Assessing its Effectiveness, Making a Construction Plan, Painting the Actual Vessel and Observing the Ship at Sea.

Working in tandem with Warner's and Loyd's departments were teams of civilian camoufleurs located at key shipping yards whose chief role was to transfer the camouflage plans onto the ships. Behrens, in an article called 'Setting the Stage for Deception…' (2016), notes that many of the camoufleurs were established artists and that while they were 'not authorised to devise their own camouflage plans (a restriction they greatly resented), they were permitted to modify a design given to them to make it fit a particular ship. The modifications were photographed and the results were then shared with higher-ups'. Warner soon realized that mistakes were being made and therefore he implemented weekly training sessions for the civilian camoufleurs in Washington, D.C. It was during one of these training sessions, when he cut up one of the ship models into blocks, that he discovered a faster means of developing a camouflage scheme.

The artist and muralist William Andrew Mackay (1876–1939) was appointed the head of the camouflage section of the Emergency Fleet Corporation's (EFC) New York District. On 16 April 1917 the EFC was established by the USSB to build ships as quickly as possible. Mackay's main task was to supervise artists applying the Dazzle patterns to the ships. The EFC ordered more than 700 Ferris ships (named after EFC's chief naval architect Theodore E. Ferris), although only around 265 of these small, coal-fired, wooden-hulled ships carried cargoes to Europe. USS *Banago* was one of the Dazzle-painted Ferris ships in service from 29 September to 21 December 1918.

In November 2012 part of a wartime essay by Henry C. Grover entitled 'Developing Methods of Ship Protection' was posted on Camoupedia. Grover was a commercial artist from Boston who had relocated to Washington, D.C., after his appointment as Camouflage Secretary of the EFC in February 1918. In the article he recounted:

> *Camouflage painting was considered so important that it became a part of the construction division of the [Emergency Fleet] corporation. A nationwide organization was built up, there being district*

(left) USS Banago was one of the Dazzle painted Ferris ships in service from 29 September to 21 December 1918. Courtesy US NHHC/U.S. National Archives.

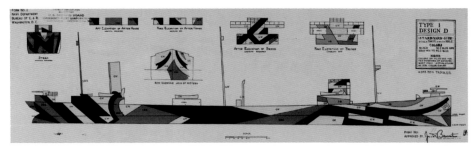

(left) Maurice L. Freedman (circa.1895–1983). The Fleet Library of the Rhode Island School of Design (RISD) has excellent examples of Dazzle ship plans by Freedman that he donated to their collection. Type 1 Design D is shown here. Courtesy the Fleet Library, Rhode Island School of Design.

camoufleurs in 11 different districts of the country, distributed according to the requirements of the work. The organization was started at the home office in Washington, D.C., under the management of Henry C. Grover, and within a short time about 150 men were actively at work and graded as district camoufleurs, camoufleurs and assistant camoufleurs. There were also subdistricts in charge of resident camoufleurs who were stationed at Portland [Oregon], Los Angeles, Norfolk [Virginia], Providence [Rhode Island], and Montreal, Canada.

Camoupedia also reveals that an Alon Bement worked in Washington, D.C., as 'a camoufleur, first class, of the United States Shipping Board'. Bement (1876–1954) had studied art in Paris and taught at Teachers' College, Columbia University, the Maryland Institute of the Arts and the University of Virginia, and that among his pupils he counted the celebrated artist Georgia O'Keeffe. Bement was invited to speak at the Senior Assembly of the Manual Training High School in early May 1919 (*Brooklyn Daily Eagle*, 6 May 1919), where he talked about his duties. He explained why transports, freighters and destroyers were camouflaged and not the battleships:

'The big fighters were not daily subject to submarine attack so that it was unnecessary to give them their "make-up" and since it costs $3,000 to paint a battleship attention was confined to the first mentioned ships.'

Bement wrote an article for the *Washington Times* (15 June 1919) entitled '"Camouflage" for Fat figures and Faulty Faces', which appeared with the strapline 'Prof. Bement Shows How the Scientific Laws of Light, Color and Pattern Can Be Applied To Your Household, Your Clothes and Even Your Features'.

During 1917 and 1918 Maurice L. Freedman (c.1895–1983) was the District Camoufleur for the USSB in Jacksonville, Florida. After the war he studied art at the Rhode Island School of Design (RISD) when he donated 455 plans and 20 photos of Dazzled ships. One photograph depicts the SS *Everglades*, launched on 29 July 1918 in Florida and the first Dazzled ship in the USA. Post-war, Freedman specialized in commercial art and developed an early version of the game 'Battleship'.

It is tempting to assume that Freedman's generous donation solves the problem of establishing the actual colours utilized to Dazzle the ships – however, Behrens states: 'There are...several hundred color lithographic plans (including one full set at the Fleet Library at RISD), but they state that the colors shown on the plans are merely placeholders and may not be the actual colors applied.' Further information posted on Camoupedia derives from an article in *The Daily Long Island Farmer* (9 January 1919) relating to the Jamaica Women's Club based in the New York City borough of Queens. Mrs J.T. Cooley was in charge of the Arts and Crafts Department and was responsible for booking the speakers, who included Henry Devonport, described as 'a portrait painter of Boston', and Thomas Benrimo, 'a magazine illustrator'. She reported that:

> These artists responded to their country's first call for camoufleurs, and as such have been working on boats [ships] in New York Harbour for many months ... It has been a tedious and most difficult job for these artists, for besides a long day at work, 7 days in the week, the boats themselves were not easy to decorate, as on one side they were unloaded of their cargoes and on the other, perhaps loaded. All the work had to be done while ships were in port and besides the loading and unloading there were the usual number of mechanics on board, cleaning, painting and repairing. ... The original plans of working were made at Washington and might not fit the boat they were designed for. Much of the actual work of painting – the large masses – was done by Swedes with huge brushes, but the marking out and finishing was done by these patriotic artists who were accustomed to much finer and more congenial work.

Behrens has collated some biographical information on Henry Davenport (1881–1965). He was a Harvard graduate who initially studied architecture in Paris before focusing his attention on painting, and he later taught art and lectured in art history at Yale University. David L. Witt's *Modernists in Taos* (2002) tells us that Thomas Duncan Benrimo (1887–1958) worked as an avant-garde artist, a magazine illustrator and theatrical designer, and he also lectured on camouflage methods. Behrens has also compiled new information on David Orville Reasoner, the son-in-law of Abbott Handerson Thayer, who was appointed as one of the camouflage artists for EFC until 15 December 1915. Also, the painter and muralist Thomas Hart Benton (1889–1975), who in the post-war era was a pioneer of the American realist

modern art movement called Regionalism.

Based at Norfolk, Virginia, Benton's duties included making visual records of the camouflage designs of ships of all countries. Henry Adams's *Thomas Hart Benton: An American Original* (1989) includes a letter from Benton to a friend that outlines war work. Benton wrote:

> I am now officially listed as [a] 'camoufleur' and I have a nice quiet room in Norfolk and an office in which to work. There are two more 'camoufleurs' in the office with me, a photographer and a young would-be artist. Twice a week I leave the office at Norfolk with the fellow who takes the photographs. We go on board a 40-foot motor boat and cruise around the bay making sketches and photographs of newly arrived camouflaged ships. The sketches are finished back at the office (the colors of the camouflage are put in) and along with reports giving name, type, tonnage, etc., of each ship are sent to Washington to be filed. This is done so that if the ship should be torpedoed or lost in any way all the facts concerning her appearance etc. can easily be found.

One of Benton's surviving visual reports is of the British ship SS *Alban* (1914) spotted in Hampton Roads in the afternoon on 30 October 1918.

The graceful steamship *Alban* was built as a passenger/cargo liner for the Amazon trade by the Caledon Shipbuilding & Engineering Company in Dundee for the Booth Line. Her normal sailing route from Britain to around 1,000 miles up the Amazon to Manaus was one that Wilkinson had experienced himself. The ship survived two U-boat attacks by torpedo on 17 June 1917 by *U-82* and on 11 May 1918 by *U-70*, as well as gunfire from the German submarine *U-152* on 24 September 1918. She was hit and sunk by Allied aircraft during the Second World War on 10 October 1941, having been sold to the Italians in 1935.

By the end of his fourth week in the USA Wilkinson visited New York 'to see a number of the camouflage officers there and to attend a Dinner of all the noted American illustrators who had done war posters'. The chairman of the American Society of Illustrators at that time was Charles Dana Gibson, who was well known at home and in Britain for his alluring creation of the 'Gibson Girl'. Wilkinson received a copy of a complimentary letter from one of the society's artist members, Henry Reuterdahl, who was attached to the

US Department of Camouflage and had originally written a letter to Admiral Sims, which he published in his autobiography:

> Commander Wilkinson, being the first one to invent a successful system of camouflage, established in France and the United States the details of his system, this by giving personal instruction to the officers concerned. Every phase of the present camouflage was worked out by Wilkinson, and what we have in our navy, as well as the designs adopted by the U.S. Shipping Board, is based entirely on his discoveries.

Because this letter is placed in Wilkinson's book immediately prior to his discussion of the controversial debate relating to his and others claims on the invention of Dazzle painting, as adjudged by the Royal Commission on Awards to Inventors (RCAI), it is clear that he had acquired it originally as supportive evidence.

Camoupedia has posted details of Reuterdahl's experiments with naval camouflage, which included the USS *De Grasse* (1918). From Lida Rose McCabe's article 'Camouflage: War's Handmaid' in the *Art World* (January 1918), it is known the artist stated, 'There is no science that I know of in my ship camouflaging' and 'I am guided wholly by feeling acquired through twenty-five years more or less buffeting the sea'. However, this insight into his working method was hardly useful advice or help for the implementation of the large number of ships that needed to be camouflaged in the USA. Sources differ in terms of whether or not the patrol vessel USS *De Grasse* (ID-1217), converted from a yacht, ever saw active service.

Wilkinson would have brought a selection of Dazzle plans to distribute to the key officials during his visit to the USA, and arranged to have others shipped over after his return home. However, after imparting his Dazzle scheme, Wilkinson's secondary objective would have been to ensure that the US subdivisions became self-reliant. In the absence of records to the contrary it can be assumed that for the most part the relationship between the artists and scientists was harmonious. It was certainly productive and effective, given the large numbers of

HENRY REUTERDAHL

Self-taught Swedish-American Henry Reuterdahl (1870–1925) was regarded in his lifetime to have been the leading marine artist working in the USA. He enjoyed a long-standing relationship with the United States Navy and became head of its poster bureau, although he was not afraid to be highly critical in public of the necessity for naval reform, particularly in its bureaucracy. For a time he was editor of *Jane's Fighting Ships*.

(above) Henry Reuterdahl (1870–1925).

(below) Henry Reuterdahl (1870–1925), Help Your Coun[try?] *U.S. Navy recruitment poster issued on 1 January 1917, prio*[r] *to the introduction of Dazzle camouflage. Library of Congre*[ss]

Philadelphia-born
WILLIAM ANDREW MACKAY (1876–1939)
studied at the City
College of New York,
the Académie Julian in
Paris and the American
Academy in Rome. He
produced murals for the
Library of Congress, the
American Museum of
Natural History and the
Minnesota State House of
Representatives.

EVERETT LONGLEY WARNER (1877–1963)
was born in Vinton,
Iowa. He worked as an
art critic, printmaker
and Impressionist
painter. His art training
included art classes at
the Corcoran Museum
and the Washington Art
Students League, both
in Washington, D.C., the
Arts Students League
in New York and the
Académie Julian in Paris.
After his return to the
USA in 1909 he became
closely associated with
the art colony in Old
Lyme, Connecticut,
that had become a focal
point for Impressionist
artists. It is also where he
met Abbott Handerson
Thayer, through the
artist Frederick Childe
Hassam. Warner was one
of the most important
US camoufleurs in the

two world wars. Several
years after his death in
1972 a fire in his former
studio destroyed many of
his drawings, paintings,
ship models, reference
notes, papers and
correspondence.

FREDERICK JUDD WAUGH
(1861–1940) was the
son of the well-known
Philadelphia portrait
painter Samuel Waugh.
His passion for the
ever-changing moods of
the sea – and especially
breaking coastal waves
as his preferred subject
– mirrors that of the
Cornish-based artist Julius
Olsson, although with
Judd the waves are more
vigorous in execution.
It is possible that they
were familiar with each
other's work. Judd, after
studying with Thomas
Eakins at the Pennsylvania
Academy of Fine
Arts and at the Académie
Julian in Paris, also lived
and worked for a time
on Sark, in the British
Channel Islands.

designs produced and the remarkable record of those ships that were Dazzle-painted and survived during the war.

The passion, commitment and effectiveness of Dazzle in the USA is recollected by George R. Havens in his biography *Frederick J. Waugh: American Marine Painter* (1969). He recounted that the artist:

> ...*threw himself into naval camouflage with all his energies, finding in this new work a ready outlet for his natural mechanical bent. Many large ships, including the 'Leviathan,' were painted according to his designs. Through the enterprise was of course a team effort in which no one man played a solo part, he had every reasons to be proud of his record. Only one ship with his system of camouflage was lost during the war.*

Initially, there was a close connection between Britain and the USA as Wilkinson recalled in his autobiography that around '1,100 American merchantmen were painted to the designs originated in the London department'. Gradually, Wilkinson's influence faded and the objective of empowering the US specialists, in terms of creating their own Dazzle designs, was achieved.

In 'Setting the Stage for Deception...' Behrens reports that American naval camoufleurs relied increasingly on their own discoveries. In particular they focused on, in Warner's words, 'reverse perspective'. Warner himself explained the principle by getting his readers to imagine a ship painted with increasingly large square shapes on the hull from bow to stern (front to back). As this is contrary to the laws of perspective, it would visually trick the submarine commander viewing the ship through a periscope. And, as he explained further, give 'the idea that the bow is farther away from us than the stern, and that the vessel is heading away, when in reality it is steering in our direction'.

Beyond the official offices of the US camouflage departments, artists were also drawn to Dazzled ships as a subject in their own right. Two in particular are worthy of mention here: Burnell Poole (1884–1939) and Arthur Lismer (1885–1969), both of whom were fascinated with the Dazzled four-funneled ocean liners of rival shipping companies Cunard and White Star Line.

Boston-born Poole packed a lot into a short life. He produced photographs, paintings and prints of maritime subjects and received commissions from the US government and worked as a naval correspondent for *Everybody's Magazine* during his travels to England in the summer of 1918. There is a website dedicated to his work (website www.pooleart.com), which is mainly in British and US collections. Two notable examples, a pair produced around 1920, show port and starboard views of the *Mauretania* (the sister ship of the ill-fated *Lusitania*), Dazzled in part with a chequer design. The paintings now reside on different sides of the Atlantic with one in the US Navy Art Collection and the other in the Merseyside Maritime Museum.

Lismer was born in Sheffield, England, and he later emigrated to Toronto in 1910. He was a member of the so-called Group of Seven artists. In 1916 he worked at the Victoria School of Art and Design in Halifax (later called the Nova Scotia College of Art), where he became the principal. By 1919 Lismer had returned to Toronto and the post of vice-principal of the Ontario College of Art. His Dazzle paintings related to his work for the Canadian War Memorials Fund and its newly established Home Work Section, which gave him a free hand to seek out maritime subjects. Lismer's best known Dazzle painting depicts the RMS *Olympic* (the sister ship of the ill-fated *Titanic*) at Halifax, Novia Scotia. It was entitled *Olympic with Returned Soldiers* and painted in 1919. This painting – along with two other Dazzle-related subjects, *Convoy in Bedford Basin* and *Convoy and Tugs* – are now in the Canadian War Museum.

(left) Arthur Lismer (1885–1969).

(above) Burnell Poole (1884–1939) Mauretania in dazzle paint, *print. Courtesy US NHHC.*

CAMOUFLAGE IN THE USA BEFORE WILKINSON'S DAZZLE SCHEME

During Wilkinson's initial meeting with Roosevelt, the ASN had been candid in his opinion on the current state of naval camouflage: 'Up to the present ship camouflage in the United States has been carried out by a number of private individuals, all of whose systems vary, but are mainly in the order of invisibility or low visibility treatment. They have been selling their plans at so many dollars a foot run to ship-owners'. And he went on to say: 'We have had no means of testing the results in a practical way and I personally regard the camouflage that is now being done as a form of "Juju black art bad man no can see".'

This certainly explains why Wilkinson's services were in demand, but is this really a fair assessment of the preceding concepts? And did any of them anticipate Wilkinson's Dazzle painting scheme?

Roosevelt's recollections related to the concepts, recommendations and schemes advanced by several men, but especially those by Everett Longley Warner who in 1917 was officially tasked to test out an earlier invention by Thomas Alva Edison (1847–1931) and the artist, naturalist and teacher Abbott Handerson Thayer (1849–1921) and his friend and fellow artist George de Forest Brush.

From 7 October 1915 Thomas Alva Edison was chairman of the Naval Consulting Board. This organization was established after the sinking of the *Lusitania* on 7 May 1915, with the death of around 1,200 passengers and crew, including 128 American citizens, to advise on military matters. In the summer of 1917 the United States Shipping Board (USSB) was given

GEORGE DE FOREST BRUSH

George de Forest Brush (1855–1941) was an American painter and art potter who collaborated with his friend Abbott Handerson Thayer on a camouflage scheme for ships. Brush's wife Mary, an artist and aviator, also contributed to camouflage schemes for aircraft. Nancy Douglas Bowditch, the artist's eldest daughter who worked as a painter and theatre designer, provides the core details of his life and work in *George de Forest Brush: Recollections of a Joyous Painter* (1970).

Born in Shelbyville, Tennessee, Brush studied at the National Academy of Design in New York, and in Paris. After returning to the USA he became fascinated by Native Americans, which resulted in remarkable illustrations and paintings derived from living among members of the Arapaho, Crow and Shoshone tribes. Bush is best known for these Native American subjects, often depicted in a neoclassical style with a heroic demeanour inspired by his Parisian tutor Jean-Léon Gérôme. He was awarded many medals for his work at national and international exhibitions and was elected to the Society of American Artists in 1880, the National Academy of Design in 1908 and the American Academy of Arts and Letters in 1910.

George de Forest Brush (1855–1941). Private Collection.

the opportunity to test out a camouflage scheme that had been invented by Edison and Warner was selected to assist with the trials.

In Nelson C. White's book *Abbott H. Thayer: Painter and Naturalist* (1951) he cites an undated letter Warner wrote in 1917 about his role in an attempt to make the former German cargo ship USS *Ockenfels* (later renamed USS *Pequot*) invisible, in part with 'a big spread of canvas', stating that it was '...a very wild idea. I know because I had the job of doing the painting work on the vessel. Part of the added camouflage structural work was so unseaworthy that it got carried away before the vessel got out of New York harbour'.

Interestingly, although an inventor universally recognized for his brilliance, Edison advanced 48 ideas to the US Navy during the war and none of them succeeded beyond testing stage. On 29 September 1917 Warner wrote to the Bureau of Construction and Repair in Washington, D.C., with his proposal for protecting ships at sea from the submarine threat. His concept echoes that of Norman Wilkinson. Behrens relates that Warner argued that it was, 'Practically impossible to make a ship invisible from a submarine, because she was almost invariably outlined against the sky and consequently would show up in silhouette', and that his proposal therefore aimed 'to break up the silhouette in such a way as to make it very difficult for the enemy to obtain the range'.

What became known as Warner's System was one of several inventions officially sanctioned by the USSB, although Wilkinson's invitation to the USA highlighted that these were not wholly successful. Other authorized schemes, as noted on Camoupedia, were devised by Gerome Brush (the son of George de Forest Brush), William Andrew Mackay, Lewis Herzog, Maximilian Toch and the American poster artist F.M. Watson. With Wilkinson's scheme already up and running, and receiving some positive feedback, the US authorities must have felt it was prudent to back his scheme rather than pump precious resources into undertaking further tests and trials on their own schemes. However, if they had fully backed Warner it is highly likely that the need for Wilkinson would have never have arisen.

Abbott Handerson Thayer was an artist and camouflage specialist. He was a complex character who appears to have been susceptible to pronounced mood swings, and may even have been bi-polar. This may have been one reason for his reputed eccentric behaviour and opinionated and mercurial manner. Boston-born Thayer initially studied with the amateur animal artist Henry D. Morse before moving to Brooklyn, New York, to study at the Brooklyn Art School and the National Academy of Design. He exhibited some works at the Society of American Artists and in 1875, after his marriage to Kate Bloede, he studied in Paris for four years at the École des Beaux-Arts, where he met his closest friend and camouflage collaborator, George de Forest Brush.

Abbott Handerson Thayer (1849–1921), Angel, 1887, oil on canvas. Courtesy the Smithsonian American Art Museum. Gift of John Gellatly.

which include countershading (also called Thayer's Law), background blending and the use of disruptive or dazzle patterns. These all predated the schemes of both Professor John Graham Kerr and Norman Wilkinson. Thayer started to develop his ideas on countershading in the early 1890s. In 1896 he wrote, 'Animals are painted by nature, darkest on those parts that tend to be the most lighted by the sky's light, and vice versa'. Countershading therefore makes animals harder to see.

Thayer provided photographic evidence to prove the efficacy of countershading in nature by showing two wooden duck decoys. The photograph first appeared in the May 1908 issue of *Century Magazine* and appeared later with a more detailed description in Thayer's book *Concealing-Coloration in the Animal Kingdom*, first published in 1909 and

After returning to New York, Thayer established a portrait practice and started to teach. Celebrated sitters across his career included the American authors Henry James and Mark Twain. In addition, he made good use of family members, especially his children Mary, Gerald and Gladys who featured in some of his most successful artworks. Mary was the model for the best known of his series of paintings of angels. Entitled simply *Angel*, it was painted in 1887 and is now in the collection of the Smithsonian American Art Museum. Thayer wrote: 'Doubtless my lifelong passion for birds has helped to incline me to work wings into my pictures; but primarily I have put on wings probably more to symbolize an exalted atmosphere (above the realm of genre painting) where one need not explain the action of the figures.'

Thayer's attempts to transform his fascination with guardian spirits into the material form of camouflage systems to protect ships at sea met with mixed reviews – and in some quarters a very hostile reception. However, Thayer's unofficial title of 'the father of camouflage' can be justified through his several important contributions,

(above) Ockenfels *(later renamed USS* Pequot) *before and after camouflage. Courtesy Roy R. Behrens (PD).*

reissued in 1918. The ducks were painted the same colour as the surrounding earth, the only difference being that the one on the left had not been countershaded. There were, not surprisingly, doubters among the magazine's readership. Thayer addressed their concerns when the photograph was reprinted in 1909, when he wrote: 'The reader will have to take it on faith that this is a genuine photograph, and that there is a right-hand model of the same size as the other, unless he can detect its position by its faint visibility...'

In 1898, during the Spanish–American War, Thayer and George de Forest Brush recommended countershading as a form of protective colouration for American ships. The war did not last long enough for the concept to be implemented, although they succeeded in patenting, on 2 December 1902, their invention of a 'Process of Treating the Outsides of Ships, etc., for Making Them Less Visible' (U.S. Patent No. 715013A). In fact, as Behrens has identified, it was Brush's son, the sculptor Gerome Brush, who applied for the patent on his father's behalf.

The patent was not put into practice because countershading in itself was not sufficient to reduce the overall visibility of a ship at sea. However, it was Thayer's research on what he called 'ruptive' marks that would have a profound impact on the development of camouflage. In *Concealing-Coloration in the Animal Kingdom* he argued that animals were concealed by a combination of countershading and disruptive marks ('ruptive' marks), which together 'obliterated' their self-shadowing and their shape. Thayer explained:

Markings...of whatever sort, tend to obliterate,—to cancel, by their separate and conflicting pattern, the visibility of the details and boundaries of form... If the bird's or butterfly's costume consists of sharply contrasted bold patterns of light and dark, in about equal proportions, its contour will be 'broken up' against both light and dark—light failing to show against light, dark against dark. Such is apparently the basal and predominant use of almost all the bolder patterns in animals' costumes.

With or without Norman Wilkinson's knowledge of these disruptive marks or patterns, they were in fact the underlying biological principles behind Dazzle painting.

Thayer's influential, and controversial, 1909 book had been brought to fruition by his son, Gerald Handerson Thayer. Critically, the publication was ridiculed publicly by some – most notably by Theodore Roosevelt, the

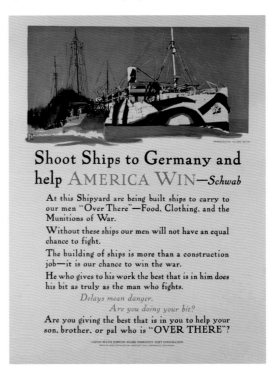

Shoot Ships to Germany and help AMERICA WIN—*Schwab*

At this Shipyard are being built ships to carry to our men "Over There"—Food, Clothing, and the Munitions of War.

Without these ships our men will not have an equal chance to fight.

The building of ships is more than a construction job—it is our chance to win the war.

He who gives to his work the best that is in him does his bit as truly as the man who fights.

Delays mean danger.

Are you doing your bit?

Are you giving the best that is in you to help your son, brother, or pal who is "OVER THERE"?

UNITED STATES SHIPPING BOARD EMERGENCY FLEET CORPORATION

26th President of the United States, who was also an author, explorer and naturalist of some repute. Thayer merely overstated his argument in asserting that all animal coloration is related to camouflage and thereby undermined his camouflage work at that time.

In *Evolution* (1926), under the section heading 'Breaking up of the Continuity of Surface: 'Dazzle' Patterns', Professor Kerr wrote:

> *Another beautiful principle which nature makes use of is that which has come to be familiar from its war uses under the name 'Dazzle'. In this she takes advantage of the psychological processes which are made use of in the act of recognition, inasmuch as she superimposes upon the surface of the animal's body conspicuous markings, which serve to concentrate upon themselves the observer's attention, and in this way enable the tell-tale colour or form of the animal to pass unnoticed. ... The principle is the same as that which makes an open lace-work curtain, or even an arrangement of white tapes pinned at considerable intervals across a window, effective as a means of preventing the casual passer-by from noticing the interior of a room.*

Although Kerr and Thayer did not always see eye to eye, they became friends. In the University of Glasgow archive there is a letter from Thayer to Kerr, dated 11 April 1914, that reveals the friendship. Thayer wrote:

> *I have the pleasantest memories of you and Cambridge and your hospitality to me there, and I often wish to connect myself with you again. My son & I got out a book on Concealing Colouration and sent many copies of it broadcast among our friends, yet I can't remember sending one to you. This seems inexplicable to me now... Will you not send me a word to say that you are still alive and to tell me where to send you a copy of the book?*

Kerr tried to help Thayer with his quest to assist the British Admiralty's camouflage schemes in the early stages of the war. Kerr noted that 'it was myself who induced Abbott H. Thayer, the American artist & discoverer of Thayer's Law – to come to Cambridge and paint the "invisible bird" which is a well-known curiosity in the Museum of Zoology'.

On 5 December 1915 Kerr wrote to Prime Minister Arthur Balfour: 'My reason for writing is that Mr. Abbott

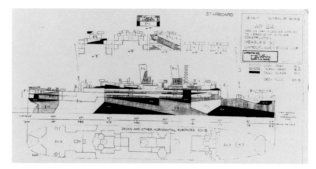

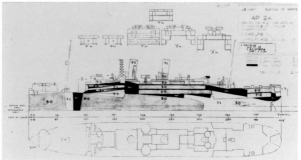

Photo # NH 101700   USS Orizaba in port, 1918

USS Orizaba *(1918) was a transport ship for the United States Navy in World War I & II. Her original Dazzle plans are shown at the top. In the photograph above she is shown departing New York via the North River for France in the First World War. Courtesy US NHHC.*

Photograph of the USS West Mahomet *in dazzle camouflage, 1918. She was a steel-hulled cargo ship built as part of the United States Shipping Board's World War I emergency wartime shipbuilding programme. However, she was completed too late to see active war service. Courtesy US NHHC.*

SS Alloway *on sea trials 5 July 1918. USS* Alloway *(1918) was a screw-steamer cargo ship built by Moore & Scott in California. She survived the war. Courtesy US NHHC.*

Built in 1918 at San Francisco as the SS Independence *and seen here at anchor, while wearing dazzle camouflage, circa 1918. This photograph may have been taken in the San Francisco Bay area, California. Courtesy US NHHC.*

USS Nebraska *(1904). The Virginia-class battleship photographed in the US Navy yard of Norfolk, Virginia on April 20, 1918 painted in experimental Dazzle camouflage. Courtesy US NHHC.*

H. Thayer a well-known American Artist – whom I mentioned in my letter to Mr. Churchill in September of last year... the discoverer of the principle of graduated shading...is now in the country and desirous of placing his services at the disposal of the Government.'

There have been several attempts in recent years to address the wide-ranging achievements of Thayer in terms of his art and his expertise in natural history and his significant contribution to camouflage, mostly notably in October 2008 when a documentary film about Thayer's life and work premiered at the Smithsonian American Art Museum. It was entitled *Invisible: Abbott Thayer and the Art of Camouflage* and it featured a wide range of his drawings and paintings, archival photographs, historic documents and interviews with Thayer's family, friends and supporters, including Professor Roy R. Behrens.

Returning to the First World War, Thayer's was one of many recommendations and proposals sent to assist the British Admiralty. But it was Professor Kerr and not Thayer who was Wilkinson's main challenger for the Dazzle Painting 'prize'.

(above) A government news photograph of members of the US Women's Reserve Camouflage Corps camouflaging the USS Recruit *in Union Square, New York City. 1917. Courtesy Roy R. Behrens (PD).*

(below) The liner Mauretania *in wartime Dazzle. This photograph inspired the Cunard artwork for the poster 'On War Service – On Peace Service' which heralded the resumption of commercial sailings after World War I. Getty Images.*

RIVALS FOR THE DAZZLE PAINTING 'PRIZE'

Wilkinson was well aware of the competing camouflage schemes during the war. This is revealed in his autobiography, in which he published a paper from Rear Admiral Greatorex, Director of Naval Equipment, that was written at the outset of the establishment of the Dazzle Section in the early summer of 1917. In the paper was a list of eight plans and recommendations in addition to Wilkinson's scheme, including a number that were trialled. A proposal from Abbott Handerson Thayer 'to paint submarines like high swimming open sea fish' was abandoned after 'a form of blue paint was tried'. A plan by Mr G.A. Clarke, 'an expert in orthochromatism', to paint ships with a horizontal graduation of blue was tested by painting HMS *Caryfort* but it proved to offer no benefit. An invention of reflecting paint by E. Dixon of Messrs Blundell Spencer & Co of Hull proved to be ineffective. Percyval Tudor-Hart (1873–1954), the artist, colour theorist and teacher, advanced a scheme of painting ships to make them invisible but it proved unsatisfactory when it was tested at Portsmouth on a motor launch.

Also on the list was Professor J. Graham Kerr's proposal '…for diminishing visibility by compensating shades destroying the continuity of outline…' but it was concluded that this scheme 'proved of little or no advantage'. However, until his death Kerr relentlessly campaigned to advance his claim that his scheme was in principle one and the same as Wilkinson's. Kerr was adamant that his concept had not been properly implemented and trialled by the Admiralty and he became the main rival in the quest for the Dazzle painting 'prize'. For Kerr and Wilkinson the stakes were high, not only in terms of the prospective monetary reward but also their public perception of their characters and professional reputation.

Herbert Barnard John Everett (1876–1949), Convoy *(1918), oil on canvas. National Maritime Museum, Greenwich, London.*

Portrait of Professor John Graham Kerr (1869–1957) by T & R Annan & Sons Ltd

Front cover of Kerr's book 'A Naturalist in Grand Chaco' Private Collection.

For 33 years, from 1902 to 1935, the distinguished academic John Graham Kerr (1869–1957) was Regius Professor of Zoology at the University of Glasgow. He was elected a Fellow of the Royal Society (FRS) in 1909 and knighted in 1939. In addition to his busy academic life (he was a 'legendary lecturer') and family commitments he was preoccupied until his death with the subject of camouflage. In 1903 he married Elizabeth Mary with whom he had two sons and a daughter; and after his wife's death in 1934, he was betrothed to Isobel Dunn in 1936. Camouflage was a passion that derived from his study and teaching of natural history but was driven forward by his total belief in his paint protection scheme for ships.

Born at Arkley, Hertfordshire, he was the son of James Kerr the well-known author and educationalist, a former principal of Hoogly and Hindu College, Calcutta, and Sybella Graham of Hollows, Dumfriesshire. Kerr, like Wilkinson, was one of four children, although he lost his mother at an early age. He was encouraged by his father to read books on exploration and natural history, which included Charles Darwin's *Voyage of the Beagle* (first published with a different title in 1839) and Alfred Russell Wallace's *The Malay Archipelago: The Land of the Orang-Utan, and the Bird of Paradise. A Narrative of Travel, with Studies of Man and Nature* (1869).

Kerr was educated in Scotland at Dalkeith, Midlothian, and for a short time at the Collegiate School, Edinburgh, then at the Royal High School. He studied higher mathematics and natural philosophy before focusing on Medicine at the University of Edinburgh. This was later followed by Natural Sciences at Christ's College, Cambridge (Darwin's old college) where he was a brilliant student, awarded first-class honours in Part II of the Natural Sciences Tripos.

Kerr's interests at Cambridge included English literature – he was secretary of the Shakespeare Society, although his greatest passion apart from natural history was boating and yachting, which he had acquired in his youth. This was reflected in his membership of the Cambridge University Cruising Club. Kerr's personal photographic albums, now in the University of Glasgow archive, depict some of his cruises around Britain and further afield, as well as photographs of racing yachts and regattas. However, it is what occurred between his studies at the respective universities that, he later admitted, 'determined the whole of my future life'.

Kerr's time at Edinburgh was cut short after picking up a copy of the scientific journal *Nature* at Waverley railway station. It featured an announcement from the Secretary of the Zoological Society of London stating that the Argentine Navy, under the leadership of Captain Juan Page, was preparing to undertake a survey expedition of the Pilcomayo, the main western tributary of the Paraguay River in south-central South America, from the Paraná in southern Brazil to the frontiers of Bolivia, the land-locked country in western-central South America.

Aged only 19 Kerr joined the party as naturalist and sailed for Buenos Aires on 2 June 1889. The party made its way to the Gran Chaco, where Kerr was given free rein to study the flora and fauna. His account of the expedition that ranged over the years 1889 to 1891 was entitled *A Naturalist in the Gran Chaco* and was first published towards the end of his life in 1950. Sailing aboard the river steamer *Bolivia*, Kerr quickly gained the confidence of the commander, who allowed him to undertake pilotage duties, and also on occasions take charge of the helm.

Edward Hindle, who superseded Kerr in the post of Regius Professor of Zoology at the University of Glasgow, summarized Kerr's abilities and personal attributes in his book *Biographical Memories of Fellows of the Royal Society*, in which he wrote:

...his field notes on the habits of a wide variety of animals including the adaptations of those living

in swamps, protective colouration [from which he developed his ideas on naval camouflage], and his observations on the Natokoi [he described them as the 'aborigines of the Chaco'] showed even at this early age that he was not only an observer and naturalist of exceptional ability, but also a man of resource, courage and endurance above the ordinary.

Tragically most of the specimens Kerr collected on the expedition were lost.

After Cambridge Kerr made a return expedition to the Gran Chaco (in 1896–1897) accompanied by fellow zoologist John Samuel Budgett, the main object of which was studying and collecting *Lepidosiren* – the South American lungfish. The fish was part of his overall research interests in morphology, and especially embryology, and he was able to bring large numbers of specimens safely home. Kerr's obituary notice for *Nature* magazine (vol.179, 8 June 1957) included the observation: '...both at Cambridge and Glasgow, the South American collections formed the subject of the greater part of his research work... The whole series of papers, on many aspects of dipnoan (lungfish) embryology, forms a corpus of research scarcely paralleled in the study of any other vertebrate.'

This expedition also enabled Kerr to formulate his ideas on camouflage. Kerr collaborated with his star student Hugh Bamford Cott, who became Lecturer in Zoology and Strickland Curator at Cambridge, on what became the influential and popular publication entitled *Adaptive Coloration in Animals*. It was first published in 1940, sold in large numbers and helped to secure Cott's academic reputation. He wrote:

We now come to what is perhaps the most interesting, and certainly the most important, set of principles relating to concealment – namely, the type of camouflage familiar to most people from its war-time uses [First World War] under the quite inappropriate term 'dazzle', and properly known as 'Disruptive Coloration'. [Kerr also refers to it as 'parti-colouring'.]

Cott also pointed out that 'it was the continuity of surface, bounded by a specific contour or outline, which chiefly enables us to recognise any object with whose shape we are familiar'. In other words to offer any sort of camouflage it was essential to break up the outline and this is achieved in nature through 'the use of *patterns*'.

He added:

... Now the patterns worn by many animals such as Giraffes and Jaguars, Anacondas and Iguanas, Pipits and Plovers, and various Grass-frogs, Grasshoppers, Moths and Mantids, operate in a somewhat analogous way. The function of a disruptive pattern is to prevent, or to delay as long as possible, the first recognition of an object by sight. ... Its success depends not only on optical principles, but upon a psychological factor. When the surface of a fish or a factory is covered with irregular patches of contrasted colours and tones, these patches tend to catch the eye of the observer and to draw his attention away from the shape which bears them.

For Kerr 'Disruptive Coloration' and Dazzle painting were one and the same thing. Both work by breaking up the outlines of an animal, ship, building, machine or soldier with a strongly contrasting pattern. It's a form of optical and visual diversion that has the potential to prevent or diminish the effectiveness of an attack.

Some of the key parts on camouflage in Cott's book were derived from Kerr's earlier work *Evolution* (1926). Kerr used his influence to secure for Cott the position of advisor on camouflage for the British Army in the Second World War, which enabled Cott to shape War Office policy, something that Kerr was so eager to do himself during the First World War.

Hugh Bamford Cott (1900–1987) in 1945. University of Glasgow.

Examples of disruptive coloration in zebras. Courtesy Shutterstock.

On 24 September 1914 Kerr wrote to Winston Churchill, First Lord of the Admiralty (1911–1915), and outlined his plans to protect ships. He put forward three suggestions, the third of which related to the need to break up the continuity of the surface of the ship with his 'parti-colouring' scheme. He wrote:

> It is essential to break up the regularity of outline, and this can easily be effected by strongly contrasted shades. The same applies to the surface generally – a continuous uniform renders conspicuous. This can be counteracted by breaking up a surface by violently contrasting pigments. A giraffe or zebra or jaguar looks extraordinarily conspicuous in a museum, but in nature, when not moving, wonderfully difficult to pick up, especially at twilight. The same principle should be made use of in painting ships.
> ... The outlines [of ships] more particularly should be broken up by patches of white ... the bow, stern, and upper lines of the hull should also be broken up with very large patches of white ... [and the] sides of the ship should also be broken up by large patches of white, and what has been said naturally applies also to turrets and other parts of the upper works.

The Admiralty was reluctant to use large amounts of white paint in the early stages, mainly because of wartime shortages, although it was later 'found to be the best "colour" for those parts of the ship intended to be invisible'. In 1922 this was recorded in the counsel notes relating to the case held by the Royal Commission on Awards to Inventors (RCAI).

Initially, Kerr's scheme was favourably received by the Admiralty. This is evidenced by a letter from the Admiralty, dated 19 December 1914, thanking Kerr for 'the valuable information' and informing him that 'the data and suggestions...have been communicated to the Fleet confidentially in a General Order'. This General Order was issued on 10 November and was headed 'Visibility of Ships – Method of Diminishing'. It also stated 'The trial or adoption of the proposals made therein is left to the discretion of Flag Officers, &c. concerned'. However, this General Order had been approved without any prior consultation with Kerr.

The Dazzler

LIEUT.-COMDR. N. WILKINSON, R.N.V.R., AT WORK IN HIS STUDIO

The success achieved by this gallant officer in beating the U-boats was entirely due to the copious experiments carried out regardless of personal comfort or his own studio furniture. The extreme secrecy of the work, moreover, proved an incessant strain

The Dazzler, a caricature of Norman Wilkinson by Reginald Higgins appeared in The Bystander magazine in February 1919. It shows the artist with his easel and furniture Dazzled to resemble zebra stripes. © Illustrated London News Ltd/Mary Evans.

HMS Argus (1918). British Aircraft Carrier, (1918–1946) photographed in a British harbour, 1918, painted in Dazzle camouflage. Courtesy US NHHC.

Some feedback from the trials was very encouraging and included a letter received by Kerr from Archibald Geoffrey, a former student then serving aboard HMS *Implacable*. He had observed a cruiser with 'irregular spatches of white dotted here and there on her hull and funnels' and considered it to be effective.

Kerr also discovered after the war, through a letter to *The Times* on 12 May 1919 from Lieutenant Colonel Maurice Gerald Holmes, former Chief of the Seaplane-Carrier Section of the Admiralty, that his scheme had been a success. Holmes wrote: '...as long ago as spring, 1915, four of His Majesty's vessels were painted in a manner corresponding very closely to modern camouflage methods, and one based upon the helpful suggestions contained in his letter [Kerr's scheme], which was circulated by the Admiralty to naval officers.'

Holmes continued: 'The present writer was informed by officers who put to sea with these vessels [which included the seaplane carrier HMS *Argus*] that the result aimed at was attained and that it was exceedingly difficult to determine the general features of the vessels when they were steaming at sea.'

Kerr's pleasure in receiving the positive reports was short-lived. The extensive correspondence in the University of Glasgow archive and library reveal the increasing frustration of Kerr in his attempts to ensure that his scheme was properly implemented and supervised.

On 14 June 1915 Kerr wrote to the Admiralty, 'it occurs to me for example that I might be of use for purposes of inspecting and advising in connection with this matter of visibility'. He repeatedly offered his services, although his written requests to Winston Churchill and Arthur James Balfour the Prime Minister were all to no avail.

On 9 July 1915 Kerr received a letter from V.W. Baddeley of the Admiralty stating 'it is not proposed to proceed with any further trials at present'. The ships were returned to their 'uniform colouration' of grey. This would become the default position of British naval camouflage.

Now frustrated, Kerr wrote to Sir George Beilby, a Fellow of the Royal Society (FRS) and a member of the Admiralty Board of Invention and Research (BIR), to seek his assistance to find out why his scheme had been dropped. The BIR had a heavy workload and from its establishment during the war to 1918 over 41,000 submissions were evaluated. Beilby believed that Kerr's scheme had significant merit and he promised to investigate further. Kerr would be disappointed again when the reason for the abandonment was relayed back to him. The Admiralty adjudged that 'the great variations in environmental conditions' at sea countered 'any beneficial effects of the special painting'.

Kerr wrote again to Churchill and Balfour but to no avail. He persisted month after month, year after year to push his case forward, arguing that the scheme had not been properly implemented and supervised, and that significant improvements could be made. In 1917 Kerr wrote to Sir John Maclay, the Minster of Shipping, but with Wilkinson already 'on board' and the Dazzle Section now up and running, Kerr's services were not required.

Indefatigable Kerr approached Sir Donald MacAlister, Principal of Glasgow University, to seek his assistance in finding out why Wilkinson's scheme had been implemented over and above his own.

After the war Kerr was prompted into a new phase of campaigning, both in private and for the first time in public. With the restrictions of wartime censorship lifted, Norman Wilkinson was the first to go public – claiming sole credit for the invention. An article appeared in *The Times* on 6 December 1918 and a version of it also appeared in the *Glasgow Herald* on the same day. The article contained this assertion:

...the originator of 'Dazzle' is Lieutenant-Commander Norman Wilkinson, the well-known marine painter of ships and the sea. In May, 1917, he submitted his scheme to the Admiralty...[his] argument was that if a ship could be broken up into strongly contrasted design her course could not be observed without longer periscope observation and even then not exactly. This delay and uncertainty might prevent the submarine getting into firing position until the ship had obtained a chance of escape.

(above) W. A. Richards (exhibited 1893–1920), HMS Ramillies as she appeared in September 1917, whilst serving with the First Division of the First Battle Squadron of the Grand Fleet, *watercolour. Courtesy of Liss Llewellyn Fine Art.*

Kerr was incensed. He wrote again to Sir George Beilby, requesting that he intervene to ensure the 'unfairness' was straightened out at the Admiralty to 'avoid any element of public controversy'. The Admiralty refused and Kerr shifted his campaign into the public arena. In May 1919 he wrote letters to *Nature* and *The Times*. On 9 May his letter to the editor of *The Times* was published in an attempt to finally, in Kerr's view, put the record straight. It included this passage:

In the highly successful camouflage of ships as it was carried out during the closing phases of the war the principle made use of was that, familiar to biologists, of breaking up continuity of surface and outline by violent colour contrasts. I happened to have become especially interested in this problem of the camouflage of ships long before the war.

He followed that with three key points:

(1). I was professionally interested as a biologist in the obliterative colouration of animals. (2) During my sojourns in the Gran Chaco during the years 1889–91 and 1896–7 I had had the extraordinary efficiency of Nature's methods of obliterative colouring constantly

brought home to me by practical experience (3).When present at the opening of the Kiel Canal in 1895, as one of the crew of Mr. W. B. Hardy's yacht Raven, I was particularly impressed by the fact that, whereas the ships of the British squadron attending the festivities retained their beautiful colouring of cream funnels and black hulls, the French and German warships on the other hand adopted an obliterative colouring of uniform grey – the shade differing somewhat in the two cases.

Kerr then summarized his observations and key points that he had impressed upon the Admiralty after the outbreak of war, which included:

...while it was not suggested that a ship at sea under average conditions could be rendered invisible in the strict sense, yet on the other it was quite feasible (a) to diminish greatly the conspicuousness of a distant ship, and (b) to stultify the enemy's range-finders by confusing the details – such as, above all, vertical lines – of which they make use. (It is unnecessary to recall that in range-finding as applied to ships at sea there are two factors involved (a) the determination of distance, and (b) the determination of the rate and direction of relative movement.) (2) That of the various methods which Nature makes use of in her obliterative colouring of animals there were two alone of practical value for application to ships (a) the contrast-colouring method already alluded to and (b) the method of compensative shading – the obliteration of relief by counteracting the light and shade to which the appearance of relief in large objects is mainly due.

And he continued:

I urged upon the Admiralty that as protection against long-range gun fire these two basic principles should be applied to the colouring of ships. The hull and the upper works were as a preliminary to be treated on the Thayer principle, dark shadows being lightened and high lights darkened, and the main protection applied in the form of strongly contrasting pigments, the boundary lines between the colours running uninterruptedly across boats, guns, turrets, &c. Of course precisely the same principles apply to ships viewed through the periscope of a submarine; but in these early days of the war the submarine menace had not yet become insistent.

Ironically, Kerr concluded: 'At last, during the summer of 1917, I had the satisfaction of seeing the principle of parti-colouring [the interchangeable term with obliterative colouring] come into its own. Discarded by the Admiralty as useless two years before, the value of the principle was now recognized and its application entrusted to skilled hands.'

Wilkinson took time to prepare his defence before submitting his letter to *The Times* on 9 June, using the address of the Royal Thames Yacht Club to add prestige to his submission. Prior to submitting his letter Wilkinson almost certainly consulted with Dr James Cecil Mottram (1879–1945). Mottram had qualified as a medical doctor in 1903 but had gone into research, and in 1914 had written *Controlled Natural Selection and Value Marking*, which considered the function of colour and pattern in natural selection. In June 1918 Mottram had been transferred to the 'Special Works School, Kensington', which was a camouflage department in London. His main contribution was his fundamental and applied work on the principles of camouflage. Mottram later corresponded with Kerr, with whom he did not see eye to eye, and wrote to *The Times* on 5 June 1919 in support of Wilkinson. Both Mottram and Wilkinson shared a passion for fly-fishing.

Wilkinson's defence was a well-studied, punchy letter of attack. He agreed with Kerr 'that the principle of obliterative colouring was no new thing, and was common knowledge to biologists'. However, he went on to say that, 'My aim in replying to his letter is with a view to showing that I was not working on biological lines, and thus remove a misapprehension'. Wilkinson continued:

I feel that Professor Kerr has not thoroughly grasped the idea of the special form of camouflage on which I was engaged, and of which I still claim to be the originator. 'Dazzle Painting,' so called officially, had one purpose in view only, Viz., to upset the submarine commander's estimate of a vessel's course when carrying out an attack with torpedo.

In Kerr's original submission to the Admiralty his plan focused on the protection of naval ships from other ships or guns (gunnery) at long range, although he also later made it clear that it could be adapted for defence against submarines. Wilkinson forced this point home:

I was under no misapprehension as to its value for gunnery, and in my original submission to the Admiralty in May, 1917, made no claim that it might be used for this purpose, as I felt certain that paint alone could not possibly have sufficient carrying power to stultify the enemy's range-finders at the great distances at which a modern action would probably be fought.

Then he started a new line of argument:

The accurate estimation of a vessel's course is the prime factor required by a submarine commander to ensure successful attack. In every dazzle design this point was studied to the exclusion of all others, i.e. to frustrate accurate calculation of course. The mere breaking up of a vessel's form by strongly contrasting colours would not achieve this end without careful study of the perspective and balance of the design. I am not aware that this occurs in biology, i.e. the disguise of direction.

And in another attempt to undermine Kerr's claim, Wilkinson argued:

Surely the obliterative colouring of birds and animals is only operative so long as the bird or animal is in a state of rest; the moment movement commences the illusion is destroyed. The ship subject to torpedo attack is in constant movement. Again, in how many cases is nature's scheme for protection successful when the subject is seen on a ridge silhouetted against the sky? Yet this is the only point of view from a submarine when observing a ship through the periscope.

Kerr did not agree with Wilkinson's view on the relationship of animals to their habitat or background, or his claim that their natural 'camouflage' offered no protection while in motion. He believed Wilkinson's opinion derived from erroneous parts in Thayer's 1909 publication. Kerr later put forward evidence to the RCAI stating that: 'A Zebra or a Jaguar is inconspicuous in the twilight quite independently to its background.'

Finally, Wilkinson rounded off with practical points that he believed undermined the use of Thayer's principle of 'compensative shading' at sea that Kerr had also advised the British Admiralty to adopt. He wrote:

I must say that after extensive observations at sea I have failed to observe any gain in this method of painting. In a letter of this length is it not possible to go into the causes of its failure; but only to state briefly one or two of the main objections. To take the practical side first, what shadows are there in our modern battleships to compensate which would retain white paint for more than a few hours? The various controls on the mast are in close juxtaposition to the funnel, and subject to constant heat and smoke. The hawse pipes are rusty after a few hours steaming, while the shadow cast by the flare of the bow is automatically compensated by reflected light thrown up from the bow wave. There is a small shelter deck amidships far too deep in shadow for any light paint to overcome.

And with respect to merchant ships:

...the same difficulties arise. No shadows cast by passenger decks can be overcome by the use of white paint, which is itself dependent on light for luminosity. These decks present a very different proposition to a bird's breast receiving reflected light from the ground or sand on which it stands, or from the glitter of water below. I am not theorizing in making these statements; they are the direct outcome of observation at sea for some years.

The public spat caught the attention of Mr E.A. Fraser Smith, the Secretary of the North-East Coast Institution of Engineers and Shipbuilders, who had asked Wilkinson to present a paper, 'The Dazzle Painting of Ships', at their Victory Meeting to be held in Newcastle-upon-Tyne on 10 July 1919. Wilkinson also delivered this paper, with some variations, to the Royal Society of Arts, London. It was published in the *RSA Journal* on 12 March 1920.

The secretary thought it would be a good idea to allow Kerr to present a paper too. Kerr declined the offer to attend and present in person, and instead he sent in a short account outlining his position that was read at the event and later published alongside Wilkinson's longer paper. In fact, Kerr turned down an offer to see Wilkinson's text before submitting his own.

Wilkinson focused on the failures of all previous attempts that used paint to protect ships. He misleadingly stated: 'All the previous attempts which have been made to utilize paints as a defensive measure

when dealing with ships were made with a view to rendering them invisible.' It was a clever and effective ploy to undermine Kerr's scheme. The salvoes against Kerr had started in the first lines of the paper, where he wrote: 'The paper I am about to read to you deals with the origin and development of dazzle painting, and I shall endeavour to show the reasons for its adoption as opposed to painting a ship with a view to achieving invisibility.' The third paragraph included: 'I shall hope to show you that so-called invisibility against submarine attack is not only impossible, but dangerous.'

Kerr's attempts to counter these claims were repeatedly unsuccessful, although an examination of the documentary evidence shows that it was never his aim to make a ship wholly invisible.

Yet again Kerr put pen to paper to advance his case. In August 1919 he wrote to Winston Churchill asking for assistance in rectifying this 'awkward and distasteful' situation. Although not known for certain, it is highly likely that Churchill encouraged the setting up of a Committee of Enquiry on Dazzle Painting to investigate the competing claims, to which Kerr was invited to attend – and he appeared before the Admiralty Patent Section at

'57, Charing Cross, London' on 11 November 1919.

The official papers and documents in the National Archives, Kew, and in the University of Glasgow archive and library reveal that that the committee became preoccupied with the mistaken belief that Kerr was advocating the invisibility of ships and it focused on the fact that Kerr's original submission related to the protection of ships from the guns of an enemy ship at long range rather than from submarines.

On 20 October 1920 the Admiralty stated that Kerr's claim had been dismissed because 'incidental resemblance is no ground on which a claim can be properly based'. In addition to Kerr's scheme, the Admiralty enquiry also threw out three other claims by Mr J.M. Baker, Captain F.M. Livingston-James of the East Lancashire Regiment and the Liverpool-based fine art dealer Archibald E. Phillips. The last two are worth addressing a little further. Livingston-James said that after corresponding with Wilkinson he went to see him at Burlington House to discuss his ideas, which he claimed had then been adopted by the Dazzle Section.

(above) Charles Pears (1873–1958), HMS Fearless, *1918, oil on canvas, Imperial War Museum (ART 1360).*

John Lavery (1856-1941), SS Appam, London Docks, 1918, oil on canvas, Imperial War Museum (ART 1281). Lavery served as an official war artist but was not part of the Dazzle Section.

Phillips later expended considerable time and money to prepare a substantial illustrated booklet entitled 'Suggestions for the Camouflage or Dazzle of British Merchant Ships in the Great War'. One design depicted a two-funnelled vessel painted overall with hexagrams. Ben Whittaker, of the National Museums Liverpool, has highlighted what he considers to be Phillips' contribution to camouflage. In his article 'Zig-zag Dazzle Ships' (Liverpool Biennial online Journal, 2016), Whittaker points out that although Phillips' scheme was not regarded as viable and was finally dismissed by the Royal Commission on Awards to Inventors (RCAI) in 1922, he had at least sent in ideas to the Admiralty before Wilkinson. Phillips wrote:

> ...the painting of a ship's hull with strong contrasts of colour and shape [that] could distort the appearance in such a way as to confuse the enemy, not to render a ship concealed or invisible (as Wilkinson claimed all other previous proposals did). His first proposal in May 1915 specifically refers to an intended dazzle effect. In this respect, his ideas were valid and pre-dated those of Wilkinson.

Whittaker acknowledges that Phillips 'does not seem to have had any scientific or military background. He had the idea – and that cannot be taken away from him – but not the ability or knowledge in the appropriate areas to translate that idea into a feasible scheme'. However, Whittaker also acknowledges that Phillips' undeveloped ideas did not predate Kerr.

The Admiralty offered Kerr a lifeline in its recommendation to approach the RCAI, an organization that rewarded those whose inventions were judged to have been of material benefit in the war. Wasting no time, Kerr submitted his claim on 15 November 1920.

Kerr had never intended to claim a pecuniary prize or reward for his scheme. However, the RCAI only dealt with monetary matters and so he submitted a claim for £10,000. In a summary of Kerr's claim, the RCAI stated:

> ...the system of protective coloration of ships commonly known by the misleading name 'Dazzle' and made use of on a large scale during the War is a system communicated by him to the Admiralty in September 1914 and he appeals to the Royal Commission to determine that this claim is just. His reason for making this appeal is that after the close of war numerous newspaper interviews and magazine articles advertised the system of 'Dazzle' painting of ships, as an invention of the year 1917 by one of the Admiralty experts Mr. Norman Wilkinson without giving any indication that the system had been in the possession of the Admiralty since September 1914.

There was plenty of time for the claimants to prepare their cases because the hearing was set to take place on 16 October 1922 at Martlett House, Bow Street, in London.

During the evidence-gathering process Kerr's correspondence reveals the frustration of himself and his supporters. One of them, Maurice Gerald Holmes, wrote to Kerr on 19 February 1920 about Wilkinson's promotional abilities in claiming Dazzle painting as solely his scheme. Holmes observed, 'Norman Wilkinson seems to be "trading" in camouflage and has – of course – done much to get it taken up. But he rather usurps the ingenuity of the Almighty'. Other documents reveal that Kerr questioned Wilkinson's character and motives.

At the outset of the Admiralty enquiry, Kerr replied to one particular question – that he recollected as 'Whether or not I suggested that Mr. N. Wilkinson had

appropriated my idea of "parti-colouring"' – with a point-form letter dated 28 November 1919:-

(1) *I cannot get over the fact that Mr. Wilkinson was a professional marine artist in pre-war days and that as a necessary consequence he must have been extraordinarily interested in all questions dealing with the appearance of ships at sea; his mind must have been peculiarly receptive to anything bizarre and strange in their appearance; he must have been extremely interested in all talk and discussions regarding anything of this kind.*

(2) *I find it extraordinarily difficult to believe that Mr. Wilkinson of all people had not become aware of the following facts. (a) The occurrence of the early Dazzled ship of 1914–1915 with their (as it then seemed) grotesque appearance. (b) The discussions and common-talk regarding these 'enormities'. (c) The existence of my memorandum – widely circulated in the fleet and (d) the publication of photographs of such ships in the press e.g. 'Sphere' August 14th 1915. Yet a knowledge of any of these would have at once made a person of Mr. Wilkinson's special ability cognizant of the principles of Dazzle or parti-colouring.*

(3) *If I assume that after Mr. Wilkinson went to the Admiralty to run the Camouflage department he remained ignorant of the existence of each one of my communications dealing with what was the special interest of himself and his department, then I find myself up against the fact that in his letter to 'The Times' of 9th June 1919 he does not state, as one would have expected, that on becoming aware of my letter to 'The Times' he had once enquired into the matter at the Admiralty and made the unexpected discovery of communications with its remarkable parallelism with his own ideas. This is the reaction which I should have expected to be produced by a letter such as mine occupying the first column of 'The Times' correspondence page and printed in big type.*

He concluded:

These are the main facts which have produced a definite impression in my own mind. But I have no personal knowledge of Mr. Wilkinson. I have had no opportunity of 'sizing him up' as a human being, and under these circumstance I feel that I might be doing

The Weymouth-class light cruiser HMS Dartmouth *(1910) Courtesy Getty Images.*

HMS E 11 *(1914) an E-class submarine. Priavte Collection.*

HMS London *(1899). Imperial War Museum (SP 1881).*

(opposite above) The Lord Nelson-class battleship HMS Agamemnon *(1906) in the Dardanelles. Courtesy: Maritime Photo Library.*

a very grave injustice to Mr. Wilkinson if I suggested that he has wittingly appropriated ideas that were not his own. I have more than once come across cases where a man has also dished up an idea due to someone else as his own, in the most absolutely honest and entirely forgetfulness of how the idea originally got into his brain.

As discovered by Kerr himself, and more recently Hugh Murphy, Honorary Professor of the University of Glasgow, and Dr Martin Bellamy, Head of Research, Glasgow Life, during research for their article 'The Dazzling Zoologist – John Graham Kerr and the Early Development of Ship Camouflage' (*The Northern Mariner*, XIX, No.2 April 2009), it remains a mammoth and challenging task to identify and assemble pictorial material of ships painted according to the 'parti-colour' scheme. Murphy and Bellamy have identified several vessels, including: the Canopus-class HMS *Canopus* (1897), the Diadem-class cruiser HMS *Argonaut* (1898), the Formidable-class battleship HMS *Irresistible* (1898), the Lord Nelson-class battleship HMS *Agamemnon* (1906) that featured as illustration in *The Sphere* on 14 August 1915, the Weymouth-class light cruiser HMS *Dartmouth* (1910) [attributed], the Indefatigable-class battleship HMS *New Zealand* (1911) and HMS *E11* (1914) an E-class submarine.

A comparison between HMS *Irresistible* and her sister ship HMS *London* (1899), coated in Wilkinson's Dazzle paint in 1918, certainly seems to support Kerr's claim (as suggested by Murphy and Bellamy) that the schemes were one and the same. Some of the vessels Norman Wilkinson encountered during his service career at sea were in fact painted according to Kerr's Admiralty submission. They included *E11* and HMS *Canopus*. Wilkinson had made drawings of these vessels and these appeared in, respectively, his own *The Dardanelles – Colour Sketches from Gallipoli* (1915) and Henry Newbolt's *Tales of the Great War* (1916)[see page 47 and illustration in chapter 3].

The second publication does not appear to have been submitted to the adjudicating committee of the RCAI. These books are certainly of interest, but do they provide conclusive proof that Wilkinson was specifically aware of and copied Kerr's scheme and that he wittingly passed it off as his own? The answer is no. In fact none of Kerr's points made a difference to the official committee. Yet again the hearing got bogged down with the issue of

invisibility, although Kerr constantly denied that his scheme aimed to make a ship invisible. He wrote:

I have never at any time admitted the possibility of painting a ship so that when at sea it would be completely invisible. What I did was to urge that the conspicuousness and recognizability of a ship at a distance could be greatly diminished, and so also with the details of the ship which are made use of in the operations of range-finding in the broad sense (i.e. the determination of distance and direction of movement).

Earlier, on 18 July 1915, Kerr had written a long letter to V.W. Baddeley of the Admiralty, explaining that:

The method which I suggested to the Admiralty aims at rendering the ship not so much invisible as unrecognisable. It admits that in whenever fashion you may colour a ship the rays from it will, under good conditions of light and atmosphere, reach for a very long distance. The object at which it aims is that these rays shall be so modified that they do not enable the observer at a distance – even if highly trained – to pick them up as a ship.

Kerr's counsel tried to get this key point across to the adjudicating committee but yet again failed.

There was a further challenge in relation to judging the claims for Dazzle painting as naval camouflage that related to the effectiveness of the scheme itself. In the last two lines of Wilkinson's letter to *The Times*, on 9 June 1919, he proclaimed that 'there can be no question that it achieved its purpose'. However, the Admiralty had reached an opposing verdict. Its enquiry, completed in October 1918, drew upon the findings of an extensive report produced on 31 July of that year in which it was concluded that Dazzle painting had little impact on the 'rates of attacks' – however, it had been 'important in raising morale among merchant seamen'. This evidence would significantly reduce the monetary award to the successful claimant.

To support his case Wilkinson called three high-profile witnesses: Admiral Sir Lewis Bayly, KCB, KCMG, CVO; Commodore Sir Bertram Fox Hayes of the White Star Line, who had commanded the Dazzle-painted RMS *Olympic* during the war; and Captain Henry George Kendall of the Canadian Pacific Steamship Company, who had survived several shipwrecks, including the torpedo attack of his ship HMS *Calgarian* (1913) by the German U-boat *U-19* off Rathlin Island, Northern Island, on 1 March 1918.

The findings of the case in favour of Wilkinson rested largely on whether he had prior knowledge of Kerr's scheme. The commission sent Kerr's lawyers a letter, which stated, 'The whole question turned on Comdr. Wilkinson stating positively before the commission that he knew nothing of Professor Graham Kerr or of his scheme of Dazzle-painting when he prepared his scheme and sent it up to the Admiralty'. Also, it referred to the fact that he 'denied that his scheme had anything to do with the colouration of animals'. He had stated that:

I supposed on any idea there are a number of people thinking on parallel lines. I certainly thought up to the very end when I heard rumours of other people claiming it, I was quite under the impression that no one had thought of this side of it, but as a marine painter with a good deal of ship knowledge one should think of that sort and be able to carry it out.

Scribbled notes in the RCAI file in the National Archives, Kew, related to Wilkinson's award of £2,000 indicate that initially £3,000 had been considered. His barrister wanted £500, but this was later reduced to £350. Wilkinson treated co-workers to a celebration at Claridge's in Brook Street, Mayfair, which was only a short walk from Burlington House.

Kerr continued to campaign. Another round of letters and heated exchanges appeared in *The Times* in March and April 1939. On 15 April 1939 Wilkinson wrote:

There are many points in Mr. Graham Kerr's letter with which I disagree; to enumerate them all would take far too long … [and since he] … maintains that he was responsible for communicating to the Admiralty the principles of 'dazzle' may I point out that among the claims for 'dazzle' painting submitted to the Royal Commission of Awards to Inventors of which Mr. Graham Kerr's was one, and where the matter was thoroughly thrashed out, my claim was the only one which received an award.

Towards the end of his life Kerr wrote a chapter entitled 'War Paint', possibly planned for an unpublished autobiography, in which he sadly reflected: 'Perhaps the most disheartening experience of my scientific life was my long drawn out conflict with the powers that be – extending over the period of the two World Wars on the utilization of certain methods of coloration well known to naturalists for the disguise of objects of importance in war.'

Kerr was possessed of a dogged determination, a personal quality shared with Wilkinson, although the latter was blessed with considerable persuasive charm. Kerr was aware he was making himself a 'nuisance' in many quarters, but he became disenchanted with his quest for fairness. Reminiscing in 'War Paint', he wrote: 'Even more to be deplored in the camouflage controversy than the nature of the replies to questions in the House of Commons – evasive, misleading, or greatly inaccurate – the consistent barring out of the scientists from positions in which they could exert direct influences upon the practical application of camouflage.' And he added that: 'I was myself barred out from membership of any camouflage committee.'

Once taken on board by the Admiralty Wilkinson was given its full backing and support, albeit there were times when he had to amend his scheme and rigorously defend it. Murphy and Bellamy concluded: 'Despite Wilkinson's claims to the contrary, it is clear that the basic principles of naval camouflage did originate from nature and that

Thayer, Brush and Kerr, not Wilkinson, had laid the foundations for the science of ship camouflage.'

In 1917, however, the concern of the Admiralty was not in origins, principles and theories but in the practical implementation of a camouflage scheme that offered some protection to ships. For Wilkinson the timing was perfect. If the threat from the German U-boats had been as grave at the outset of the war as it had become by 1917 then perhaps Kerr would have been given the opportunity to refine and adapt his scheme, and to ensure that it was properly tested and implemented. If so it is possible that Kerr rather than Wilkinson would now be credited and remembered as the inventor of the naval camouflage scheme, albeit a scheme with a different name.

(below) Kenneth Denton Shoesmith (1890-1939), Dazzled merchantman in New Orleans harbour, 1918, watercolour. Private Collection. Denton left a career in the merchant navy in 1918 to specialise in maritime painting and poster art.

(overleaf) Geoffrey Allfree (1889–1918) A Dazzled oiler with escort, 1918, oil on canvas, Imperial War Museum (ART 567). The artist was commissioned by the IWM to paint this and other marine subjects, although he was not part of Wilkinson's team.

RETURN OF 'DAZZLE' IN THE SECOND WORLD WAR

In his autobiography, Wilkinson recalled:

In 1939, when the war clouds were gathering I felt it was possible I might be able to make some use of my knowledge of ship camouflage...I therefore approached the Admiralty and saw the Captain in charge of the Trade Division. He said at once that the Admiralty were not proposing to do any merchant-ship camouflage since all vessels would be in convoy and it was therefore unnecessary.

In fact, as Wilkinson notes , 'the Admiralty did later set up an organization to camouflage war vessels'. How Wilkinson felt about its change of tack he does not reveal, however he accepted an earlier offer from the Air Ministry to advise it on the camouflage of aerodromes; and he was made 'an Honorary Air Commodore and appointed Inspector of Camouflage under the Directorate of Works'.

If Dazzle painting had been an overwhelming success in the 1910s there is no doubt that Wilkinson would have been enlisted at the outset of the war to supervise its implementation. There was also a belief in some quarters that whatever value the scheme once possessed, it was diminished in the face of increasingly sophisticated technology such as rangefinders, radar and aircraft. It was virtually impossible for a ship to hide from an aircraft.

Since the First World War Dazzle painting had evolved and changed in terms of its colours and camouflage designs. The exciting, extravagant, wacky, weird and wonderful designs gave way to a more conservative scheme that was usually described by the more pedestrian name of 'disruptive camouflage'. Some camouflage designs were inspired by and can be associated with Dazzle, but they also were distinct from it. They were created not just to protect ships from submarines but also guns at both short and long range fired by other ships.

Eric Ravilious (1903–42) Leaving Scapa Flow 1940 *watercolour © Bradford Art Galleries and Museums, West Yorkshire, UK Bridgeman Images. Note the disruptive camouflage on the upper works of the ship. Ravilious excelled as a painter, printmaker, illustrator and designer.*

Wilkinson's oil painting of the Queen Elizabeth-class battleship HMS *Malaya* (1915), produced as part of his 'War at Sea' (Second World War) series, shows the similarity of the disruptive camouflage scheme to that of Dazzle painting. The ship has large diagonal bands of blue, grey and white painted across her hull. However, in Wilkinson's painting whatever protection the scheme offered would have been neutralized by the copious amounts of smoke emitting from her funnels that would have given away her position to an enemy submarine. That said, under different weather and lighting conditions it is possible that the camouflage could work. HMS *Malaya* initially served on convoy duty in the Mediterranean and later survived – in bad light – a torpedo attack from *U-106* on 20 March 1941, around 250 miles west–northwest of the Cape Verde Islands.

Other ships were given limited or no camouflage protection. They included the armed merchant cruisers HMS *Jervis Bay* (1922) and HMS *Rawalpindi* (1925), which were coated only in grey paint. The ships were sunk by the Germans on 5 November 1940 and 23 November 1939, respectively. Both vessels were also painted by Wilkinson as part of his 'War at Sea' series.

Today visitors to London can experience a camouflaged ship of the Second World War in the shape of the light cruiser HMS *Belfast* (1938). In 1978 this vessel formally became a branch of the Imperial War Museum and was moored in the Pool of London, open to the public. She has been repainted in her disruptive camouflage scheme of the 1940s.

As the war progressed the Directorate of Camouflage (Naval Section) was formed and by 1940 it was based at the Old Art Gallery (Avenue Road) in Leamington Spa, Warwickshire. This was supported by a team from the city of Bath, as around 4,000 staff had been evacuated there from Whitehall. At Leamington Spa

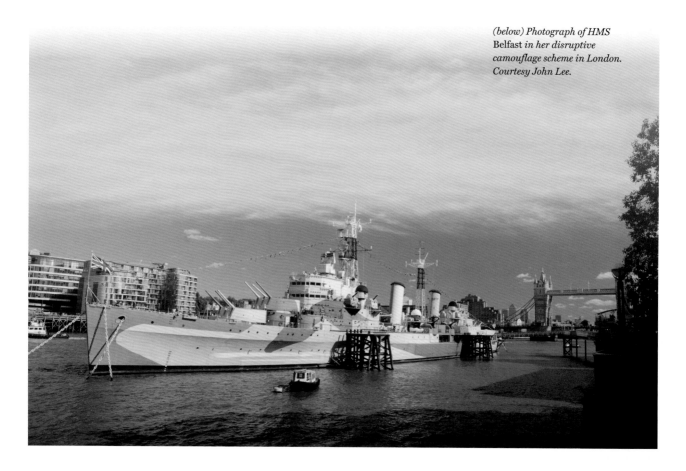

(below) Photograph of HMS Belfast *in her disruptive camouflage scheme in London. Courtesy John Lee.*

CLAUDE MUNCASTER

Sussex-born Claude Muncaster (1903–1974) worked as maritime and landscape painter, printmaker, illustrator, writer and lecturer. A self-taught artist, he started his career initially as a landscape painter at the age of 15. The son of the artist Oliver Hall, he first exhibited at the RA under the name of Grahame Hall, which he later changed by deed poll. Muncaster was an Associate of the Royal Watercolour Society (1931) and a full member from 1936; also a founder member of the Society (later Royal) of Marine Artists in 1939, and later its president from 1958 to 1974. An avid deep-water sailor and a Cape Horner his experiences were published in *Rolling Round The Horn* (1933), which he wrote and illustrated.

Claude Muncaster (1903–1974), Convoys in Peril, wash on paper. Liss Llewellyn Fine Art. Produced shortly after the war and intended as an illustration for an unidentified publication.

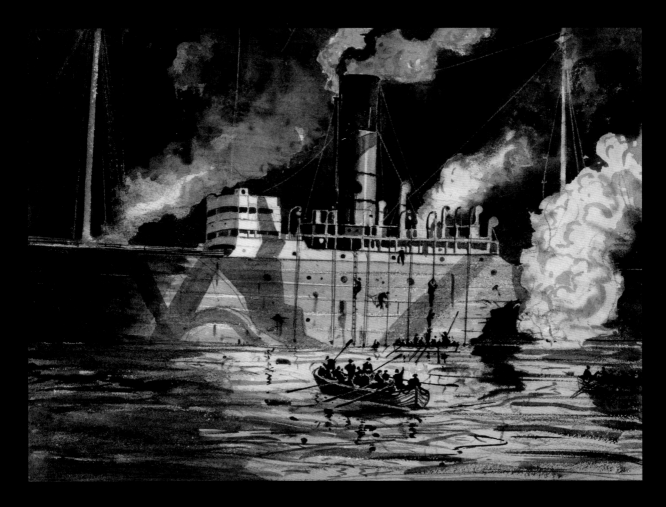

the tank testing for the painted ship models and artists themselves were based at the art gallery beside the library. The research focus was on a wide range of camouflage techniques and applications.

The camouflage officer of the Naval Section was Captain Lancelot Myles Glasson (1894–1959). He had studied at Heatherley's School of Art and the RA Schools. He exhibited regularly at the RA and became well known for his paintings of rowers. In the First World War he served as an officer in the Royal Fusiliers and lost a leg. One of the artists working there was Claude Muncaster, whose son, Martin, compiled the 'life, work and philosophy' of his father published as *The Wind in the Oak* (1978). From this book it is possible to glean some fascinating insights into the personalities and temperaments of the personnel working in the Directorate of Camouflage.

Muncaster was wary of the director of camouflage, Lieutenant Commander John Erskine James Yunge-Bateman (1897–1971), who considered him to be 'a trespasser on his preserves'. After the war Yunge-Bateman returned to his work as an author and illustrator. Muncaster admired Yunge-Bateman's charming deputy, Gerald Trice Martin (1893–1961), who was also an artist and charming. He wrote, '…if any of us wanted to know quickly the outline of a warship and the arrangements of the armaments, he would produce a perfect little outline in a matter of minutes'. Muncaster recalled that:

> There was about a dozen of us at Leamington, male and female. The team also included Wilfred Shingleton [1914–1983], the film designer, who was a superb draughtsman and a great asset to our Design Section... In the land camouflage section we had the painters Cosmo Clarke [1897–1967] and Tom Monnington [1902–1976] who was to become President of the Royal Academy.

In addition, at various times the architects and designers David Pye (1914–1993), Robert Yorke Goodden (1900–2002), Stuart Russell Matthew (1912–1996), Dick Russell (1903–1981) and Basil Spence (1907–1976) all worked in the Directorate of Camouflage (Naval Section). Pye assisted Muncaster with a 'mountain of paperwork' and had 'an incisive mind which cut through the tangle of any problem'. He later became Professor of Furniture Design at the Royal College of Art. Russell was

the 'brother of Sir Gordon Russell', the English designer, craftsman and educationalist who '…had an enquiring mind and a gift for asking disquieting questions. On the rare occasions when we thought we were doing rather well, he would bring us down to earth with a bump. He became responsible for camouflage of Coastal Forces and a very good job he made of it'. Goodden had a scientific background was 'quiet-spoken, humorous and cultured. He could write minutes which were a delight to read. An Admiralty Fleet Order which he compiled on Camouflage of Ships at Sea almost approached a literary work'.

Goodden's obituary in *The Guardian* on 26 March 2002, by the cultural historian Fiona MacCarthy, observed that he was a 'tall, shy, charming, vaguely patrician man with an enormous breadth of erudition and great human sympathy'. He was a lifelong champion of the Royal College of Art where he was professor of silversmithing and jewellery from 1948 to 1974, and he defended the 'Art' of the college by advocating that 'good design was fundamentally good art'.

Goodden had firmly believed that blue was the best camouflage colour to cope with all the varied lighting conditions encountered by the merchant service and Royal Navy. He advocated the 'strongest purest blue obtainable' and among the vessels he experimented and painted was HMS *Berwick* (1926), a County-class heavy cruiser. However, the effectiveness of blue in naval camouflage was never fully verified.

Other naval camouflage workers included the maritime author and illustrator Stanley Rogers (1888–1961), who was born in Washington State in the USA but lived in England until after the war; the marine painter Leslie Arthur Wilcox (1904–1992); the popular poster artist Fred Taylor (1875–1963); Stephen Bone (1904–

1958) who following his father's example (Sir Muirhead Bone) became an official naval war artist and W.O. Spike, Helen Rae, Una Smith, Felicity Fisher and Victorine Anne Foot (1920–2000). Fisher and Foot are both known to have worked as junior technical assistants (JTAs).

In 1993 Foot was interviewed by Angela Weight, former Keeper of the Department of Art at the Imperial

(opposite bottom) Preparing a background to test a camouflage scheme for a model warship at the naval research laboratory at Leamington Spa. Getty Images.
(opposite top) HMS Berwick *(1926), a County-class heavy cruiser at a buoy in*

the Hamoaze. Imperial War Museum (FL 1905).
(above) Victorine Anne Foot (1920–2000), Camouflaging a cruiser in drydock 1943, *oil on canvas. Imperial War Museum (ART 3016).*

(right) Frank H. Mason, The Model Maker's Shop, Directorate of Camouflage (Naval Section) Leamington Spa, oil on panel. Imperial War Museum (ART 2755).

(below) John Erskine J. Yunge-Bateman The Outside Viewing Tank: Directorate of Camouflage, Naval Section in 1943, oil on canvas. Imperial War Museum (ART 2759).

(opposite below left) Unknown artist, Britain's Sea Power Is Yours! 1945, poster. Imperial War Museum (PST 14019). [see caption page 6 for further details].

(opposite below right) HMS Kenya (1939), a Crown Colony-class cruiser. Nicknamed the 'Pink Lady' because of her 'Mountbatten pink' camouflage. Imperial War Museum (FL9253).

War Museum, which is available to listen to online. It covers Foot's wartime work there as a JTA from 1941 to 1945. She recollected among other things her art training at the Central School of Art that was interrupted because of the war. She described the experiments with camouflage patterns on ship models in the water tank, her daily routine and work duties that involved transferring camouflage designs from ship model onto paper and delivery to the Admiralty; also how ship models were removed when the ships were sunk. Foote later married the sculptor Eric Schilsky (1898–1974), who she had first met in the unit. Foote doesn't recall Muncaster, probably because he was one of the established artists she refers to who disapproved of the younger staff members (she joined at the age of 21) taking up the privilege of travelling around Britain during the quiet periods of work to paint pictures as part of a commemorative war scheme.

Frank H. Mason, the veteran camouflage officer, also made an impressive contribution. His painting *The Model Maker's Shop: Directorate of Camouflage (Naval Section), Leamington Spa* in 1943 depicts one of the modellers at work.

Yunge-Bateman, the man in charge of camouflage, produced a painting titled *The Outside Viewing Tank on the roof of the Directorate of Camouflage, Naval Section* in 1943. There was also an indoor tank with a sophisticated viewing range created by the General Electric Research Laboratories. A studio film projector supervised by Shingleton created sunlight and fan machines simulated waves. The optical system and apparatus to simulate weather conditions was designed by the scientist Dr Alphonse E. Schuil, who died during observation trails in a submarine off the northwest coast of Africa in 1943.

Muncaster recalled that Yunge-Bateman was working on disruptive camouflage and also the problems he and the team faced in making it work. They were the same challenges Wilkinson had faced earlier and had tried unsuccessfully to solve. Muncaster wrote that disruptive camouflage was designed to:

> ... confuse the outline of a ship when viewed from the air or at sea, but predominantly from the air. It was to be admitted that from an aircraft a ship would almost certainly be spotted on account of her white wake. The object, therefore, was not to make her invisible, which was virtually impossible, but unrecognizable. It was appreciated that because of the changing angles and lighting, a ship was far more difficult to disguise than a static object on land, but parts of her could be made to vanish when they matched a background of sea at

a given time. It was assumed that some seven to nine tones of grey, varying between black and white (colour shades were of no account) would by and large, be sufficient to cover the variety of times which would be met with in nature.

Muncaster went on to explain that this was fine in theory when trialled in the testing tank at Leamington Spa, but quite a different matter when put into practice at sea. He observed that 'the artist boffins, were apt to paint a ship to a corresponding tonal background and then switch on the most effective lighting condition. Nature was not necessarily going to oblige so easily'. He also said of Frank H. Mason that he:

> ...constructed the tank on much the same lines as the one he had made in World War I to test Dazzle Painting Camouflage for which Norman Wilkinson had been responsible. Mason also made models. He was certainly wasting his great talents in making our crude camouflage models, but he never complained.

Muncaster had his doubts about the usefulness of disruptive camouflage, however he noted that Yunge-Bateman and his deputy 'really did believe in the efficacy' of the scheme. Muncaster stated:

> I was rather more reserved about my faith in it. Clearly there was something in the idea, but there were limits to working in a tank, and we had to get

the Admiralty to let us try out our designs on ships at sea. They agreed trials on two ships, H.M.S. Queen Elizabeth and H.M.S. Suffolk, and I found myself responsible for carrying out these trials. But it would be some time before the ships would be ready.

Time was not on the side of disruptive camouflage. The maritime historian Brian Lavery noted, in *Churchill's Navy: The Ships, Men and Organisation, 1939–1945* (2006), that many British ships in British waters remained dark grey several months into the war and those on foreign stations were painted light grey. He also noted that 'Mountbatten pink' was also trialled but 'proved to be far from effective'.

Mountbatten pink is a colour invented by and named after the Admiral of the Fleet, Lord Mountbatten (1900–1979). In 1940 while escorting a convoy carrying war supplies he observed that a ship of the Union-Castle line with its characteristic lavender mauve grey coloured hull would seemingly disappear from sight at twilight. Convinced that this was the ideal camouflage colour, he instructed that all destroyers of his flotilla were to be repainted. It was also applied to other ships in 1941. However, as reported by David Williams, in *Naval Camouflage, 1914–1945: A complete visual reference* (2001), the Admiralty concluded that Mountbatten pink was 'neither more nor less effective in sea-going camouflage than neutral greys of equivalent tone'. In fact,

it could hinder rather than help concealment because around midday the colour became highly visible. By the end of 1942 all destroyers and larger vessels had dispensed with the colour altogether.

Other camouflage schemes were implemented that focused on reducing the visibility of ships at sea, which was something that Wilkinson had always maintained was not feasible. One scheme introduced by Peter Scott (1909–1989) – then a young naval officer, later the celebrated ornithologist, conservationist, wildlife artist and sportsman – was determined by the Admiralty to be a success. Initially, Scott served in destroyers in the North Atlantic followed by taking command of the First Squadron of Steam Gun Boats (SGBs) against German E-boats in the Channel for which he was awarded the Distinguished Service Cross for bravery. His scheme derived from Abbott Handerson Thayer's countershading principles. In July 1940 Scott succeeded in camouflaging the destroyer HMS *Broke* (1920) according to his concept, with different designs for each side of the ship.

Peter Forbes outlines Scott's scheme in *Dazzled and Deceived: Mimicry and Camouflage* (2009). On the starboard side the ship was painted blue-grey all over, but with white in naturally shadowed areas as countershading. Whereas on the port side the ship was painted 'in bright pale colours to combine some disruption of shape with the ability to fade out during

the night, again with shadowed areas painted white'. And that 'under a cloudy overcast sky, the tests showed that a white ship could approach six miles (9.6 km) closer than a black-painted ship before being seen'. The success of the scheme in reducing the visibility of the ships resulted in the accidental collision of several vessels, including HMS *Broke*. After testing at Leamington Spa, by May 1941 all ships in the Western Approaches (the area of the Atlantic Ocean immediately to the west of Britain) were ordered to be painted in Scott's camouflage.

The Admiralty introduced additional Standard patterns of camouflage in May and November 1943 – however, as Lavery concludes, 'by this time the whole concept of camouflage was coming into question and radar was beginning to make it redundant. Ships were now to be painted in light grey again, with a blue or grey patch in the central part of the hull'.

'DAZZLE' RETURNS TO THE USA

Early in 1941 Everett Longley Warner wrote to the United States Navy to offer his services. It's a story comparable to Wilkinson because his offer was declined on the grounds that there were no immediate plans to use disruptive camouflage. However, by the summer of 1942 Warner was requested to take up the appointment of chief civilian aide to his old friend and fellow artist Commander Charles Bittinger (1879–1970). Bittinger had worked under Loyd A. Jones at the Eastman Kodak laboratories during the First World War because his personal interests were in both art and science.

Warner was given every assistance to develop camouflage schemes, or what were officially called 'measures', and each one was designated a unique number. In Roy R. Behrens' publication *Ship Shape: A Dazzle Camouflage Sourcebook* (2012) he features photographs of some of the personnel who assisted Warner in developing the designs. They included Bennett Buck, Arthur Conrad, Arthur Q. Davis, Robert R. Hays, Sheffield Kagy, Eliot O'Hara and William Walters.

Some of the testing to identify suitable colours for the measures predated Warner's appointment. During the war some colours endured and others evolved, changing

(opposite) *Royal Navy cruiser HMS* Suffolk *on Arctic patrol displaying disruptive camouflage in June 1941. Imperial War Museum (A 4168).*

(above) *The U.S. Navy escort carrier USS* Santee (1939), *probably taken on 16 October 1942. Santee was the only one in her class ever camouflaged in Measure 17. Courtesy US NHHC.*

(middle) *The Omaha-class light cruiser USS* Concord (1921) *is a good example of the 'Atlantic two-tone'. Private Collection.*

(below) *The Gleaves-class destroyer USS* Hobson (1941) *painted with measure 15 off Charleston, South Carolina, 4 March 1942. Courtesy US NHHC.*

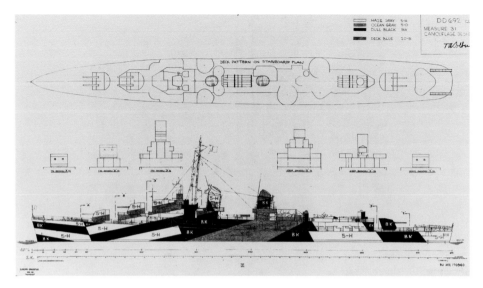

(left) Allen M. Sumner-class destroyer USS Collett *(1944) in measure 31. Drawing prepared by the Bureau of Ships for a camouflage scheme intended for destroyers of the DD-692 (Allen M. Sumner) class. Courtesy US NHHC.*

(below) USS Northampton, *a heavy cruiser of the U.S. Navy, commissioned in 1930, sunk in November 1942. Note the false bow wave. Courtesy US NHHC.*

in nature and/or name. In addition to 'Ocean Gray', colours were introduced from successful trials in the Pacific and they included 'Sea Blue' (later became darker) and 'Sapphire Blue', also 'Haze Gray' and 'Ocean Blue', in conjunction with a different colour for the upper works that included 'Deck Blue'. Testing paint colours ran in tandem with that of camouflage designs – and colours were tailored to where the ship would be serving in the world.

Measure 12, for example, in its modified form featured irregular patches and splotches resembling the arbitrary splatter of paint. Measure 15 was a Dazzle-inspired pattern that derived from the British Admiralty scheme, and it was applied to at least three vessels: the South Dakota-class battleship USS *Indiana* (1941), the

Gleaves-class destroyer USS *Hobson* (1941) and the oiler USS *Tallulah* (1942) in 1942.

Measure 17 was a Dazzle-inspired 'pattern of blues, grays and whites' that was applied to the Northampton-class cruiser USS *Augusta* (1930), the escort carrier USS *Santee* (1939) and the oiler USS *Chicopee* (1941). It was the prototype for the more ambitious Dazzle-inspired designs measures 31, 32 and 33. Measure 31 was applied to the Allen M. Sumner-class destroyers USS *Collett* (1944), USS *De Haven* (1944) and *Evans* (1944), and the medium-sized landing craft such as *LSM 152* (1944); Measure 32 to the Brooklyn-class light destroyer USS *Honolulu* (1937) and the Benson-class destroyer USS *Farenholt* (1941); and Measure 33 painted onto the New Orleans-class cruiser USS *San Francisco* (1933).

The Dazzle-inspired designs were not the most popular or widely used camouflage schemes. One of the most widely used in Atlantic and European coastal waters – from the latter part of 1942 to the end of 1944 – was Measure 22 where 'Navy Blue' was used on the lower section of the hull's continuous deck with 'Haze Gray' above. The Omaha-class light cruiser USS *Concord* (1921) is a good example. It was commonly called the 'Atlantic two-tone'.

Other means of camouflage recalled the First World War schemes in the painting of a false bow wave (also used by British ships) to give the impression that a stationary vessel was underway. Additional schemes derived from the work of Abbott Handerson Thayer that aimed at low visibility. They included Measure 16 that featured white with large polygonal patches of light sea blue (known as Thayer Blue), which was particularly effective in the Arctic.

DAZZLE IN GERMANY AND JAPAN

Strategically, the focus on the German Imperial Navy in the First World War was not on camouflaging their ships and submarines but on the wide-scale attack of their enemy. Numbers, stealth and surprise were initially on their side. However, the Second World War ushered in a new approach – as highlighted by David Williams in *Liners in Battledress* (1989) and John Asmussen and Eric Leon in *German Naval Camouflage. 1939–41*, vol.1 (2012).

All the authors state that a considerable proportion of the official German records were destroyed in the war. Williams recounts the German camouflage tests undertaken by scientists in the early 1940s, supported by the Picture-Technics Department of the Universum Film Company in Babelsberg. Camouflage designs were tested under the supervision of Dr A. Kochs by painting them on to '20cm-long [eight-inch-long] ship stencils which were then set up on a synthesized seascape in a carefully constructed viewing gallery where they were studied and photographed by diffused 'daylight".

Asmussen and Leon, in their in-depth publication, divide German camouflage into four categories: Concealment Colouring, Disguise, Disruptive Colouration and Mimicry. Dazzle camouflage and Splinter camouflage – a 'scheme characterized by long, thin, sharp edged bands of various colours that obfuscate the form of a warship at sea' – were both part of the 'Disruptive Colouration' category, or what Professor John Graham Kerr called obliterative colouration and parti-colouring. Williams describes 'Disruptive Colouration' as when 'the ship uses spots, stripes or other patterns to "break up" its outline, making targeting more difficult for any attacker' and this immediately brings to mind the schemes of both Kerr and Wilkinson. During her active service the German battleship *Tirpitz* (1939) simultaneously wore both 'splinter' and 'dazzle' camouflage. She was sunk by the Royal Air Force on 12 November 1944 off Håkøy Island near Tromsø, Norway.

The German troopship *Goya* (1940) was also painted with splinter camouflage. However, on 16 April 1945 she was torpedoed and sunk by the Soviet submarine *L-3* off Rixhöft (now Cape Rozewie) on 16 April 1945 with the loss of more than 6,000 lives.

A secret report compiled by Captain Charles Greene Grimes of the United States Navy, entitled 'Camouflage of Japanese Ship and Naval Installations', was issued in December 1945. It concluded that the 'Japanese took little interest in camouflage until the latter half of the war, when their strategic position stimulated interest in camouflage'. Like British and American ships at the outset of the war, Japanese vessels 'were for the most part painted plan gray'. However, 'elaborate concealment and camouflage was carried out on ships in port, but although all instances of this were done on much the same principles, no standardized system or doctrine was ever developed'.

The report went on to note that 'Dazzle painting was not used on Japanese warships and only on a few auxiliaries and merchantmen early in the war'. And that those 'few ships painted with dazzle patterns were painted according to the captain's personal ideas and no general orders for such painting were issued'. The Japanese certainly realized that Dazzle painting 'might be more or less effective in the daylight' but was 'extremely conspicuous at night under searchlights' and so 'never made widespread use of this technique'. It was in time concluded that the best camouflage scheme to protect the Japanese navy ships from submarine attack was the use of 'standard color number two, a shade of olive green'.

The small number of vessels that were Dazzled were for the most part 'ships whose function required their lying at anchor for much of the time, such as repair ships, seaplane tenders, etc. Many such examples of camouflage were copies of patterns seen in pictures of foreign ships, or the results of the captain's imagination'.

Lieutenant Commander Shizuo Fukui is a notable example of a Japanese naval officer who designed and supervised the painting of ships with camouflage at Singapore in 1942, prior to the instigation of official research in Japan that did not begin until 1943. The first ship he instructed to be painted was the seaplane tender *Sagara Maru*. Others included the cargo-passenger ship *Kiyozumi Maru*, the tanker *Ishiro*, the seaplane tender *Akitshushima* and the repair ship *Asabi*.

INSPIRATIONAL AND DECORATIVE DAZZLE

In Paul Atterbury's article 'Dazzle Painting in the First World War', published in *The Antique Collector* (April 1975), he noted that by the end of the war:

> *Wilkinson was not unaware of the decorative qualities of dazzled ships. In 1918 Wilkinson was commissioned by the Director of the recently established Imperial War Museum, recently opened in 1917, to paint a series of pictures illustrating the development of dazzle, and wrote, in his letter of acceptance: 'I shall be pleased to paint the pictures referred to, providing the Committee agrees, showing the characteristic phases of the form of camouflage known as dazzle painting which I originated. In addition to the two pictures discussed (A Dazzle Convoy at Sea [&] A Division of Dazzled Warships) I suggest a third as follows: this subject which would be of considerable interest would show the London Docks, Royal Albert as a good instance, which have been completely altered in appearance by the number of dazzled ships. A grey one is rarely seen now. The colours of all the ships is a most interesting and striking subject for a picture'.*

Of the three, only the 'two pictures discussed' were completed, most likely because of financial constraints. Their full titles are given as *A Convoy of Dazzled Ships in the Channel* and *Dazzled Ships at Night* and indicated on the IWM's website as 'Imperial War Museum, Art Section commission' both painted in 1918.

Dazzle captured the public imagination. *The Daily News* of 5 March 1919 featured a selection of three Dazzled costumes of guests at 'The Great Dazzle Ball of the Chelsea Arts Club'. This was featured under the heading 'The Passing Shows'. Whereas on 22 March of the same year the *Illustrated London News* (*ILN*) and its 'special artist' Samuel Begg (1854–1936) brilliantly captured the frivolity, fun and amicable chaos of the ball that was held at the Albert Hall in London, with guests in violently clashing patterns of Dazzled attire. Sir Bruce

Gretchen Vitamvas Dazzle 2, *2005, ink, collage, acrylic on paper. Courtesy the artist.*

Ingram, the proprietor of the *ILN*, considered Begg 'a marvel who could produce a picture of the London Lord Mayor's Banquet in 24 hours showing the building and recognisable principal people'.

The double meaning of 'The Passing Shows' would have been well understood at the time as a reference to the popular US musical revue 'The Passing Show' that had first started in 1894 and played on Broadway from 1912 to 1924. Adaptations and variations of it appeared in Europe and among the famous songs first sung in the series were *Pretty Baby* (1916) and *I'm Forever Blowing Bubbles* (1918). One photograph now in the collection of the National Library of Scotland, also headed 'The Passing Shows', demonstrates the influence of Dazzle on dances and stage shows. It depicts the celebrated actress and singer Miss Lee White performing at the Ambassadors Theatre in London with her Dazzle Costume Chorus. Born in Louisiana, White (1886–1927) visited England in 1913 and stayed for many years, enjoying hit performances that included *Cheep* (premiered April 1917) in which she played a character resembling Bruce Bairnsfather's 'Old Bill'.

The husband and wife photographic team of Bertram Park (1883–1970) and Yvonne Gregory (1889–1970) collaborated on a series of exuberant fashion images in 1919 inspired by Dazzle painting that feature Yvonne as the model. They married in 1916 and together they set up a studio in Bond Street, London. Bertram became one of the leading high-society photographers.

By the late 1910s and early 1920s Dazzle designs found their way onto women's swimwear, as revealed in photographs of Dazzle-camouflaged swimsuited women on the beach at Margate, Kent, in England. Different versions appeared on 15 June 1919 in the *New York Tribune* and in the following month in the *New York Sun* on 15 July 1919.

Around the same time, Roy R. Behrens identified another photograph that was reproduced in newspapers in the USA and Canada, including the Society Section and Woman's Magazine of *The Winnipeg Tribune* on Saturday, 16 August 1919.

The fascination with Dazzle fashion continues up to the present day with Alexander McQueen's Menswear Spring/Summer 2016 collection launched in 2015. The promotional material proclaims that there is 'a fresh theme found in the existence of warships that use Dazzle Camouflage, popular during World War One, to confuse the enemy about speed and direction. Vorticist artists

(left) Norman Wilkinson, A Convoy of Dazzled Ships in the Channel, *oil on canvas, 1918. Imperial War Museum (ART 4030).*

(right) Simon Begg (1854–1936), The Chelsea Arts Club 'Dazzle' Ball, 1919 at the Albert Hall, London, Illustrated London News, *22 March 1919. Illustrated London News Ltd/Mary Evans.*

(above right) Yvonne Gregory in a Dazzle costume worn at the Chelsea Arts Ball in the Albert Hall by Bertram Park (1883–1972), featured in the lower left of this cover of The Sketch magazine, 5th March 1919. Park was a successful photographer who counted the British Royal Family among his clients. He was married to, and a business partner, with Yvonne Gregory. Illustrated London News Ltd/ Mary Evans.

worked on painting the ships and some of the suiting in the collection are inspired by them'.

The public interest in Dazzle during the First World War was further stimulated through illustrated articles in upmarket art magazines – a good example being Hugh Hurst's 'Dazzle-Painting in War-Time' published in *International Studio* (September 1919), in which he shared with his readers his first-hand experiences of seeing Dazzled ships. He recollected that the ships were:

> *...resplendent with a variety of bright-hued patterns, up-to-date designs of stripes in black and white or pale blue and deep ultra-marine, and earlier designs of curves, patches and semicircles. Take all these, huddle them together in what appears to be hopeless confusion, but which in reality is perfect order, bow and stern pointing in all directions, mix a little sunshine, add varied and sparkling reflections, stir the hotchpotch up with smoke, life, and incessant movement, and it can safely be said that the world 'dazzle' is not far from the mark.*

Another novel example of the influence of Dazzle painting on land in photographic form was featured by Atterbury in *The Antique Collector*. It was first published

(right) By the late 1910s and early 1920s Dazzle designs found their way onto women's swimwear as revealed in photographs of Dazzle-camouflaged swim-suited women on the beach at Margate, Kent in England. Different versions appeared on 15th June 1919 in the New York Tribune and in the following month in the New York Sun on 15th July 1919. Courtesy Roy R. Behrens (PD).

(below) The 'Dazzle Room' art installation created by Shigeki Matsuyama at the Room 32 fashion and design exhibition in Tokyo in February 2016. Shuji Kajiyama/AP/Press Association Images. Press Association.

in the *Illustrated London News* and showed a fleet of motorized cafés in the early 1930s painted with Dazzle designs and staffed by retired naval officers. Camoupedia also addressed the same photograph and revealed a short news notice about it in the *Progress Review* (La Porte City, Iowa, 15 June 1933), which reported that in Britain:

> *A scheme for a fleet of these has been worked out as a means of providing employment for retired naval officers. These traveling cafes are really super coffee stalls, fitted out with the most up-to-date equipment for providing refreshment for hungry wayfarers. The first of them are already on the road and may be recognized by their blue and white exteriors, in the style of the wartime 'dazzle' camouflage for merchant ships.*

Since the Second World War Dazzle has inspired and influenced aspects of contemporary art, architecture and even the painted designs of motor racing cars, sports and fashion shoes. Kristian Goddard is one of many contemporary artists inspired by Dazzle camouflage. Based on North Carolina's Crystal Coast he combines a passion for art, graphic design and music. For four years he worked as an art and design lecturer at South Nottingham College in England. In his own words, he writes: 'My love and understanding of visual aesthetics and contemporary art & design have led me from graduation with honours in Graphic Design into a decade of creative, collaborative, and directorial roles. My work with filmmakers, publishers, musicians, illustrators, and artists continuously inspires me to further explorations in visual media.'

Goddard completed his second in a series of Dazzle camouflage canvases in February 2012. One of the paintings measures 60in by 40in (153cm by 102in) and was created with acrylic on canvas. He wrote on his blog:

> *...the composition is based on a detail of a dazzle ship photograph by Allie Wojtaszek. The colours derive from original dazzle ship drawings...In a perfect world I would be happy to keep working on dazzle camouflage paintings for the rest of my life! I love the modernist nature of the patterns and the use of colour, which seems very much of its time. ... I seem to be getting more and more obsessed with dazzle ships and their history after working on these recent canvases and researching the subject. Dazzle ships are quite*

> *a romantic notion to me and the idea of beautifully coloured ships floating over the water in the dark is the sort of warm thought that puts me to sleep at night.*

He also recalled, 'Peter Saville [the English art director and graphic designer] famously used Edward Wadsworth's 1919 painting *Dazzle Ships In Drydock At Liverpool* [National Gallery, Canada] as the inspiration for the Orchestral Manoeuvres in the Dark *Dazzle Ships* album cover (1983).

Brooklyn-born Michelle Weinberg works in Miami and New York as an artist and designer. Her painting projects focus on surface design, interiors and architecture. She studied at the Tyler School of Art, Temple University, Philadelphia, and the School of Art, Carnegie Mellon University, Pittsburgh. Her work *Intricate Pattern Overlay* was painted onto the exterior of the Wolfsonian-FIU Museum in Miami Beach, which is described on the website The Chromologist as: 'Referencing the stunningly Modern-looking Dazzle Camouflage, developed to disguise ships during World War I, her version uses vibrant colours to transform it into something more playful in an unexpected location.'

Charles Mary Kubricht has a long list of awards and solo shows to her name and many works in public and corporate collections. Studies at the University of Houston, Queens University in Charlotte, North Carolina, and in Vienna were followed by teaching in Houston. Kubricht draws inspiration from the Dazzle designs, especially those of the First World War that featured black-and-white zebra-like stripes. Two notable examples of her interior and exterior design work include *The Figure is Always Ground*, for the Marfa Book Company (2012) in Marfa, Texas, and the *Alive-nesses: Proposal for Adaptation*, an installation on the High Line at West 30th in New York that ran from September 2011 to November 2012. The High Line, also known as the High Line Park, is a 1.45-mile-long (2.33km) New York City linear park built in Manhattan on an elevated section of a disused New York Central Railroad spur called the West Side Line.

Kubricht painted black-and-white disruptive patterns on park storage containers, altering the view of these large structures from the northern end of the High Line. It gave the artist:

> *...the opportunity to play with the intrinsic geometry of objects using her large black-and-white geometric compositions. Positioned within the elevated cityscape*

(all images) Michelle Weinberg, an artist and designer whose projects in painting are applied to the realms of surface design, interiors and architecture. Her work Intricate Pattern Overlay was painted onto the Wolfsonian-FIU Museum in Miami Beach. "Referencing the stunningly Modern-looking Dazzle Camouflage, developed to disguise ships during World War I, her version uses vibrant colours to transform it into something more playful in an unexpected location. Courtesy the artist.

Kristian Goddard, a
contemporary artist inspired by
Dazzle camouflage.

(right) Astarboard, 2012, acrylic
on canvas.

(below) Ballast 02, 2015
acrylic on canvas.

Courtesy the artist.

provided by the High Line, the artist's treatment of the park storage containers distorts their appearance and translates the act of viewing them into a heightened visceral experience. This technique invites the viewer to move and change directions, altering familiar visual information and questioning the objects' shape and form, as well as the viewer's field of vision.

Other notable artists inspired by Dazzle include the New York-based artist Gretchen Vitamvas whose fascination with the subject started with 'reworked GAP advertisements'. In addition to paintings and drawings her work also includes live dancing models clad in camouflaged clothing. She explains that the 'uniform-like quality of the clothing and impassive, frontal presentation of the models suggested that they be revealed as soldiers. Using the clothing colors as a guide, the environments became the camouflage pattern, the process a literal blending in, which brought up themes of conformity and loss of self.' Some of her artworks feature Dazzled dancers against the backdrop of a Dazzled ship. In addition Stephanie Syjuco, Assistant Professor of Sculpture at the University of California, Berkeley, has created black and white camouflage fashion garments and accessories that were in part inspired by the World War I Dazzle designed liner SS *Leviathan* (1913).

The exterior of cars featuring Dazzle designs has long fascinated the self-taught artist Patricia van Lubeck. Born in Amsterdam, she now lives and works in the Bay of Plenty on the North Island of New Zealand. In 1990 she painted a striking black-and-white scheme on an Opel Kadett and also a Fiat Ritmo Dazzle Art Car. On her blog page, 'Dazzling Array of Art Cars', she acknowledges:

There's a good article about art & camouflage (featuring the Opel Kadett) on the Tate Museum site. An excellent source of info is the book 'Dazzle painting' by Albert Roskam. It's written in Dutch but it has lots of images. I gave my cars this urban camouflage to maximize my chances of survival in the inner city traffic.

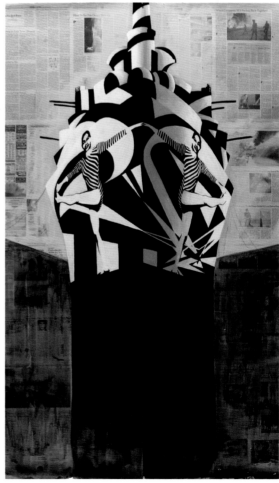

Gretchen Vitamvas (above) Dazzle Dress *and (right)* Dazzle, *2003, ink, collage, acryllic on paper. Courtesy the artist.*

CHARLES MARY KUBRICHT

(top) Alive-nesses: Proposal for Adaptation. *Installation on the High Line, New York, NY September 2011 to November 2012. See pages 107 and 111.*

(above left and right) The Figure is always Ground, *for the Marfa Book Company, Marfa, Texas 2012. See pages 107 and 111. Courtesy the artist.*

race track with Red Bull Formula One racing cars coated with 'Dazzle livery'. When Christian Horner, the manager of the team, explained the introduction of the new design scheme he revealed that it was inspired by the helmet worn by Sebastian Vettel at the Italian Grand Prix at Monza in 2014, and he remarked:

> *...new camouflage livery is a striking mixture of black-and-white stripes, which in theory makes it harder for rivals to see the details of the new RB11. It is a concept first used by the British Admiralty and US Navy in the first and second world wars to help conceal the size, distance and heading of ships from the enemy. It has since been used extensively by road car manufacturers while testing new models. ... To see a Red Bull in a different livery is quite striking and it also makes it quite difficult to get detailed photographs of the car at a time of year when we're all trying to be as secretive as we possibly can. It's difficult to get detailed shots of the car because it confuses your eye-line, but it obviously had a great reaction.*

Nike launched the sale of black-and-white sports shoes and snowboarding boots, some with red laces, as part of the 'Nike SB 'Dazzle Collection' in December 2014. The promotional material encouraged customers to 'Flummox potential foes with the Nike SB Dazzle Collection' and acknowledged:

> *...the latest offering from Nike SB presents you the chance to rep a true wonder of military history. Inspired by the irregular intersecting geometric shapes painted on military ships during World War I dazzle patterns were used to disrupt enemy rangefinders and mislead as to the vessel's true position. To confuse rather than to conceal.*

Meanwhile the American company Venus Fashion Inc. brought out the 'Two tone platform heel' inspired by black-and-white Dazzle camouflage in 2014 to coincide with the centenary commemorations of the First World War.

OPEL
(top) Patricia van Lubeck, Opel Kadett painted in 'Dazzle' design, 1990. Courtesy the artist.

RED BULL
(above) Formula One racing car with 'Dazzle livery', 2015. Getty Images

NIKE
(below) Nike Dunk High Premium SB "Dazzle", 2014 Courtesy Nike.

CENTENARY DAZZLE

Five vessels in Britain have been 'Dazzled' to mark the four-year centenary commemorations of the First World War (1914–1918). In chronological order of construction they are: HMS *M33* (1915), HMS *President* (1918), *Edmund Gardner* (1953), *Elektra* (1953/54) and *Snowdrop* (1959).

HMS *M33* is an M29-class monitor of the Royal Navy built by Workman, Clark & Co in Belfast. She is one of only three surviving Royal Navy warships from the Gallipoli campaign and was present in support of the British troops at Suvla Bay where Norman Wilkinson was on active service. In 2010 an extensive programme of restoration started, which included the reintroduction of her Dazzle-painted camouflage. After her completion she became part of the National Museum of the Royal Navy in Portsmouth on 7 August 2015, close to HMS *Victory*.

HMS *President* was built by Lobnitz & Company at Renfrew on the River Clyde in Scotland. In 1918 she was originally named HMS *Saxifrage* and launched as a Flower-class anti-submarine Q-ship. Of the 120 ships of this class, each with a different Dazzle camouflage, 18 were sunk in action. By 1922 her name had changed to HMS *President* and she was moored as a Royal Navy Reserve drill ship on the River Thames, where she is now permanently berthed by the Embankment close to Blackfriars Bridge. In 1982 she was sold to private owners and is now available for hire for conferences and functions. Rather than restore the ship to her original Dazzle colours the owners commissioned the German artist Tobias Rehberger to create a unique wraparound Dazzle-inspired design as part of the 14–18 NOW programme. Rehberger is a German sculptor 'whose work blurs the boundaries between design, sculpture, furniture-making and installation'. The scheme appears to draw upon the architecture of the Centre Georges

Sir Peter Blake
Snowdrop *(1959) formerly the*
MV Woodchurch. Everybody
Razzle Dazzle. *Getty Images*

(left) HMS Saxifrage, later HMS President in Dazzle paint, 1918, Private Collection, and repainted (below) as a Centenary Dazzle ship in 2015 by Tobias Rehberger. Keith Larby/Alamy Stock Photos.

Pompidou in Paris and the Lloyd's building in the City of London, mixed with machine elements from the modern art movement of Purism.

The *Edmund Gardner* (1953) and *Snowdrop* (1959) were also part of the 14–18 NOW centenary programme. Both ships were built in Dartmouth by Philip and Sons Ltd, who also built ferries and lightships for the Mersey, and designed by the naval architects Graham and Woolnough of Liverpool. The first named is a former pilot cutter built for the Mersey Docks and Harbour Board, which was responsible as the Liverpool Pilotage Authority, and had her built as the second of a new generation of large diesel-electric-powered cutters to replace the pre-war steam cutters. The *Edmund Gardner* and her two sister ships were all named after chairmen of the Board; the other two were the *Sir Thomas Brocklebank* (Number 1) and *Arnet Robinson* (Number 3).

The working life of the *Edmund Gardner* was around 30 years. She was purchased by the Merseyside Maritime Museum in 1982 and is now the largest object in their collections. As part of the First World War

HMS M33 *(1915), also known as* HMS *Monitor M33 (above) courtesy Wikipedia Commons and (left) Museum of the Royal Navy Press Office.*

commemorations in association with Tate Liverpool
and in partnership with the Merseyside Maritime
Museum she has been 'Dazzled' by the Venezuelan
Kinetic and Op artist Carlos Cruz-Diez, who has covered
the vessel with bright multicoloured dazzle artwork
with the assistance of painters from Cammell Laird. The
title of the work is *Induction Chromatique à Double
Fréquence pour l'Edmund Gardner Ship*. She was opened
to the public in June 2014.

From her launch until her major refit in 2003 the
diesel-powered Mersey ferry *Snowdrop* was originally
called MV *Woodchurch*. Named after a post-war housing
development in Birkenhead her original livery of
orange and black was based on that of the Birkenhead
Corporation. In January 2015 she was Dazzled by the
English Pop artist Sir Peter Blake in a project co-
commissioned by the Liverpool Biennial, 14–18 NOW
and Tate Liverpool, in partnership with Merseytravel and
National Museums Liverpool. He called it *Everybody
Razzle Dazzle*. Blake is best known for his earlier graphic
creation with a Liverpool association, the sleeve design

for The Beatles' album *Sgt. Pepper's Lonely Hearts Club Band* in 1967. Blake's design borrows elements and patterns applied to the original Dazzle scheme such as arcs, diagonal lines, semi-circles, saw-teeth and zebra stripes, as well as chequer-board patterns mixed together in his quirky, colourful and vibrant Pop art style.

The Dazzling of the former US Army Transportation Corps' tug *Elektra* in the Channel Islands is no less a remarkable achievement and the most authentic of the group of vessels in terms of Dazzle camouflage that relates to the First World War. For many years the Jersey-based artist Ian Rolls saw the vessel languishing in St. Helier harbour. She was originally built at the yard of the Olson Corporation on Lake Beresford in Florida. Rolls approached the owner with a 'view to doing something creative'. Eventually, with funding from the World War One Centenary Working Group's Art & Community Fund, which was administered by the Jersey Arts Trust, eventually the vision became a reality.

Rolls's inspiration for the design came from his interest in a particular type of Dazzle camouflage. He liked the designs that 'played visual tricks with light and shade and distorted form rather than simply using bold shapes and colours'. He goes on to explain:

> ...the design evolved using a limited palette of black, white and two shades of grey. The introduction of a red stripe in two shades which spirals around the superstructure and the hull, added a vibrant colour note which was all the more effective for its contrast with the otherwise limited palette.

With the assistance of a team of local artists, part of the Skipton Art Series 2015, the Dazzle painting was completed in June 2015.

In 2015 Wilkinson's Dazzle painting scheme was given a new lease of life in a commercial initiative instigated by the Imperial War Museum (IWM), home to the lion's share of his Dazzle-painted models, sets of plans and also many other paintings, drawings, prints by other artists and vessels by various photographers. The commodification of Dazzle is expressed in the IWM's range of black-and-white Dazzle merchandise, which includes mugs, postcards, pouches, tape, tea towels, tote bags, travelcard holders, T-shirts and wrapping paper, also limited edition prints. They were inspired in part by the zebra-like Dazzle designs painted on HMS *Kilbride* (1918), one of 54 Kil-class patrol gunboats.

The winter 2015 issue of *Despatches*, the magazine of the Friends of the IWM, featured a promotional article to formally launch the range, in which the IWM's Buying Manager Laura Mullins recounts:

> ...the IWM London reopened in July 2014 with a brand-new Atrium and First World War Galleries. The revitalized museum also saw the opening of several newly designed retail spaces showcasing many new and exclusive ranges. The IWM buying team strive to ensure that the products sold in the shops are relevant to our world-class collections, selecting and developing items for our visitors to take home after their visit. One of the IWM's most striking new ranges draws inspiration from the iconic dazzle camouflage patterns painted to disguise and protect ships during the First World War. ... For this very special project the IWM team chose to collaborate with award winning pattern design specialists PATTERNITY, the range entitled 'Fleet of Dazzle' launched at London's Design Junction in September 2014 ... is now available in IWM shops.

PATTERNITY, according to its own website, was founded in 2009 by art director Anna Murray and surface designer Grace Winteringham. Their projects are driven by the core belief that a shared engagement with pattern can have positive and powerful results. The company aims at: 'Blurring boundaries working with individuals, specialists and institutions alike across the worlds of fashion and interiors to art, architecture and science, food and drink to technology and education.' With an impressive client list that includes Apple, Bompas & Parr, the BBC, the Barbican, Celine, Clarks Originals, Diageo, the Foreign and Commonwealth Office, Getty Images, Granta, Levi's, Nike, Selfridges, the School of Life and the V&A, they can now add the IWM. Comprising a pattern-focused research and consultancy department, PATTERNITY were, according to Laura Mullins, 'the perfect partners for the project, working closely with the IWM's curators and historians on researching the theory of dazzle in order to design this striking range'.

(opposite) Examples of the Dazzle products in Imperial War Musuem shop by PATTERNITY

CONCLUSION
DID DAZZLE REALLY WORK?

In Archibald Hurd's chapter 'Dazzle Painting' in History of the Great War: The Merchant Navy (Vol. III, 1929) he reported the official conclusions of the Admiralty committees of enquiry into the effectiveness of Dazzle painting.

Early Admiralty inquiries into the efficacy of Dazzle painting concluded on 15 April 1918 with a minute from the First Lord of the Admiralty stating that 'no conclusive case for or against this confusional device has been made out,' and that 'it seemed hardly possible to arrive at a conclusion unless the actual working of the device is scrutinized over a considerable period, and the results collated after conference'.

Therefore a Committee on Dazzle Painting was established with the following four instructions:

To consider in detail the results from dazzle painting so far as then collected; to consider each month the results of dazzle painting as collected; to conduct investigations as to the circumstances under which the various designs give certain results; and to report what their conclusions are, and whether, in their opinion, the results justify the time and labour involved.

A report was produced on 31 July 1918 that recommended the discontinuation of Dazzle-painting warships, also that ships sailing in the Scandinavian convoys were to be repainted in dirty white. This was agreed. However, section 'B' of the report concluded:

...the statistics do not prove that it is disadvantageous, and in view of the undoubted increase in the confidence and morale of Officers and Crews of the Mercantile Marine resulting from this painting, which is a highly important consideration, together with the small extra cost per ship, it may be found advisable to continue the system...

On 7 September 1918 a Fleet Order was drafted with instructions to continue the Dazzle painting scheme with the agreed revisions, although it was subject to the final say of Lord Maclay, the Minister of Shipping. On

3 October 1918 his department placed on record their formal approval to continue Dazzle painting.

Hurd also wrote:

As was to be expected, the adoption of dazzle painting by Great Britain excited considerable interest among the Allied maritime nations. The adoption of dazzle painting by foreign nations came, however, too late in the war for any definite conclusions to be drawn from their experiences. The end of the war left dazzle painting still in the experimental stage, with results too meagre for future guidance. From the many conflicting opinions expressed the following results emerge:

1. *Dazzle painting has certain advantages for merchant ships, and no disadvantages save the very small extra cost.*
2. *Dazzle painting has certain advantages for warships operating alone, but is disadvantageous for others.*
3. *Its efficiency as a means of minimising successful submarine attack to an appreciable extent is not established by the evidence collected during the war.*

An unfortunate error occurred in *The Times* on 6 April 1921 in a notice headed 'Dazzle Painting Cost'. It was announced that, 'A report of the Comptroller and Auditor-General on the Appropriation Account of the Receipts and Expenditure for the Ministry of Shipping, issued yesterday as a White Paper states that the gross expenditure amounted to £104,956,384'. What the notice failed to mention was that this figure also included the cost of the construction of some of the ships. The cheapest cost of one of the older dreadnoughts was around £1,600,000.

In 1922 the entry on 'Naval Camouflage', written by Wilkinson, in the *Encyclopaedia Britannica* stated that around 4,000 merchant vessels and upwards of 400 war-vessels engaged principally in convoy and patrol duties were painted, and the total cost of painting amounted to £2,500,000, a sum that is closer to the mark.

Hurd also stated:

[an] advantage enjoyed by dazzle painting as a defensive measure was its comparatively small cost. The ships had in any case to be painted at intervals, and it was found that the work could be done satisfactorily during loading and unloading in port, with little delay, and in many cases without any

delay at all. The plan selected was laid out on the hull and upper works of the ships. The Government at the outset bore the first cost of painting, and two-thirds of the cost in the case of renewals, for all requisitioned vessels. The extra cost of dazzle painting merchant vessels came approximately to £125 per vessel on an average. On the basis of renewal twice a year, the additional cost was assessed at something between £250 and £800 per ship per annum.

Behrens has posted on Camoupedia parts of his research work on the efficacy of Dazzle camouflage in the USA. Tests started shortly after the end of the First World War in 1919 and were led by Leo S. Blodgett a student in the department of Naval Architecture and Marine Engineering at the Massachusetts Institute of Technology (MIT). His experiments and studies involved three sets of observers focused on Dazzle-painted wooden ship models tested on equipment actually used by the Boston-area camouflage artists during the war. His tests were also described and illustrated by Behrens in *Ship Shape* (2012). Of the 24 ship models observed, 12 (digitally reconstructed by Behrens) were identified as having 'the highest average error rates in course estimation'.

In other words Blodgett's results 'offered the most persuasive proof' that Dazzle camouflage was effective at misdirecting enemy torpedoes. This is also supported by the claim of the US Navy that less than 1 percent of those ships painted with naval camouflage were sunk by the enemy during the war. Although why this success rate cannot be applied to British Dazzled ships remains an unanswered question.

Dr Sam Willis, in the online BBC guide entitled 'How did an artist help Britain fight the war at sea?', raises a fascinating point in terms of the usefulness of 'Dazzle camouflage' for modern land-based protective schemes. He wrote, 'the effectiveness of Dazzle camouflage was never scientifically proven in the First World War, however, that does not mean that the scheme cannot play a significant role on modern battlefields'.

Willis highlights the current pioneering research being undertaken by the School of Experimental Psychology from the University of Bristol, which has found:

...that Dazzle can alter the perception of speed, as long as the target is moving fast enough. Participants saw two moving patterns on a computer screen, one plain and one dazzle. They were asked to estimate which was travelling faster. There was a reduction of around seven per cent in the perceived speed of some high contrast dazzle patterns. This would not have made a difference to a WW1 U-boat commander hunting slow merchant ships. But it could make a difference today where handheld rocket propelled grenades are fired at short range against moving vehicles.

Dr Nick Scott-Samuel, who led the study, explained: 'In a typical situation involving an attack on a Land Rover, the reduction in perceived speed would be sufficient to make the grenade miss by about a metre. This could be the difference between survival or otherwise.'

Norman Wilkinson packed an enormous amount into his long life and this was marked with the publication of his autobiography, *A Brush with Life*, in 1969 during his 90th year. His last painting was exhibited at the RA in 1970. No doubt if he was around today Wilkinson would have enjoyed seeing the commercialization of his Dazzle scheme.

To achieve all of this required a combination of application, persuasive charm and resolve, alongside sheer hard work, networking skills, dedication and determination. To a large extent today, Wilkinson remains an underappreciated artist. Something of Wilkinson's light-hearted humorous nature is revealed by his inclusion in his autobiography of the Dazzle ditty, written by the composer Gordon Frederic Norton (1869–1946), one of his closest friends with whom he shared a love of the St. John's Wood Arts Club.

Wilkinson was one of the 'painter-men with a sense of fun'.

Captain Schmidt at his periscope,
You need not fall and faint,
For it's not the vision of drug or dope,
But only the dazzle-paint.
And you're done, you're done, my pretty Hun.
You're done in the big blue eye,
By painter-men with a sense of fun,
And their work has just gone by.
Cheero! A convoy safely by.

BIBLIOGRAPHY

Adams, Henry. Thomas Hart Benton: An American Original. Alfred A. Knopf: New York, 1989.

Anon. British Vessels Lost at Sea, 1914–1918, HMSO: London, 1919.

Asmussen, John and Leon, Eric. *German Naval Camouflage. Volume One: 1939–41*. US Naval Institute Press, Annapolis, 2012.

Atterbury, Paul. 'Dazzle Painting in the First World War' in *Antique Collector*, April 1975.

Baker, Jean. *A Marine at Gallipoli on The Western Front: First In, Last Out – The Diary of Harry Askin*. Pen and Sword: Barnsley, 2015.

Behrens, Roy R. *Art and Camouflage: Concealment and Deception in Nature, Art and War*. Cedar Falls, Iowa: North American Review/University of Northern Iowa, 1981.

Behrens, Roy R. 'The Art of Dazzle Painting' in *Defence Analysis*, No.3, 1987.

Behrens, Roy R. 'The Theories of Abbott H. Thayer: Father of Camouflage' in *Leonardo*, No.3, 1988.

Behrens, Roy R. 'Blend and Dazzle: The Art of Camouflage' in *Print 45*, No. January/February 1991.

Behrens, Roy R. 'Camouflage' in Jane Turner (ed.), *The Dictionary of Art*. London and New York: Grove Dictionaries, 1996.

Behrens, Roy R. 'The Role of Artists in Ship Camouflage during World War I' in *Leonardo*, Vol.32, No.1, 1999.

Behrens, Roy R. *False Colours: Art, Design and Modern Camouflage*. Bobolink Books: University of Northern Iowa, 2002.

Behrens, Roy R. *Camoupedia: A Compendium of Research on Art, Architecture and Camouflage*. Bobolink Books: University of Northern Iowa, 2009.

Behrens, Roy R. (ed.) *Ship Shape – a Dazzle Camouflage Sourcebook: An Anthology of Writings About Ship Camouflage During World War I*. Dysart, Iowa: Bobolink Books, 2012.

Behrens, Roy R. 'Setting the Stage for Deception: Perspective Distortion in World War I Camouflage' in *Aisthesis* (2016).

Bement, Alon. '"Camouflage" for Fat figures and Faulty Faces' in *Washington Times*, 15 June, 1919.

Bowditch, Nancy Douglas. *George de Forest Brush: Recollections of a Joyous Painter*. Peterborough, NH: William L. Bauhan, 1970.

Black, Jonathan. 'A Few Broad Stripes – Perception, deception and the Dazzle ship phenomenon of the First World War' in Nicholas J. Saunders and Paul Cornish (eds.), *Contested Objects: Material memories of the Great War*. Routledge: Oxford, 2014.

Bryant, Ken. *The Jan and Cora Gordon pages*. http://www.janandcoragordon.co.uk/

Cooley, J.T. 'US Camoufleurs: Thomas Benrimo and Henry Devonport' in *The Daily Long Island Farmer*, 9 January 1919.

Cork, Richard. *Vorticism and Abstract Art in the First Machine Age: Origins and Development* (Vol.1). University of California Press: Berkeley and Los Angeles, 1976.

Cott, Hugh Bamford. 'Camouflage in Nature and War' in *Royal Engineers Journal*, December 1938.

Cott, Hugh Bamford. *Adaptive Coloration in Nature*. Methuen: London. 1940.

Cuppleditch, David. *The London Sketch Club*. Alan Sutton: Stroud, 1994.

Evans, Glyn L. *Dazzle-Painted Ships of World War I*. Bernard McCall: Bristol, 2015.

Everett, John. *Wicked Devils, Wicked Devils, 1945*. Unpublished autobiography held in the National Maritime Museum, Greenwich collections.

Forbes, Peter. *Dazzled and Deceived: Mimicry and Camouflage*. Yale University Press, New Haven, 2009.

Gimple, René (John Rosenberg, tr.). *Diary of an Art Dealer*, Farrar Straus and Giroux: New York, 1967.

Goodden, Henrietta. *Camouflage and Art: A Design for Deception in World War 2*. Unicorn Press: London, 2007.

Gordon, Jan. 'The Art of Dazzle-Painting' in *Land & Water* magazine. 12 December 1918.

Gordon, Jan. *Modern French Painters*. The Bodley Head: London, 1926.

Gordon Jan and Bateman, Henry Mayo. *Art Ain't All Paint*. Feature Books: London, 1944.

Greenwood, Jeremy. *The graphic work of Edward Wadsworth*. Wood Lea Press: Woodridge, 2002.

Grimes, Captain Charles Greene. 'Camouflage of Japanese Ship and Naval Installations' in US Government Secret Report, December 1945. See: http://www.fischer-tropsch.org/primary_documents/gvt_reports/USNAVY/USNTMJ%20Reports/USNTMJ-200K-0022-0089%20Report%20X-32.pdf

Hartcup, Guy. *Camouflage: A History of Concealment and Deception in War*. Charles Scribner's Sons: New York, 1980.

Havens, George R. *Frederick J. Waugh: American Marine Painter*. University of Maine Press: Orono, 1969.

Hewison, Robert. 'Cutting and Dazzling: Edward Wadsworth, Vorticism and Woodcuts', a paper presented at the Vorticist International Symposium, 29 January 2011.

Hurd, Archibald. 'Dazzle Painting' in the *History of the Great War – The Merchant Navy* (Vol.III, *Spring 1917 to November 1918*). John Murray: London, 1929.

Hurst, Hugh. 'Dazzle Painting in War-Time' in *The Studio*, September 1919.

Kerr, John Graham. Archive of John Graham Kerr's correspondence concerning camouflage and related material, including personal papers and family photographs. Unpublished. University of Glasgow's Archive and Library. Reference: GB 0248 DC 006.

Kerr, John Graham. *Evolution*. MacMillan: London, 1926.

Kerr, John Graham. *War Paint.* Unpublished memoir in the collection of the University of Glasgow.

Kerr, John Graham. *A Naturalist in the Gran Chaco.* Cambridge University Press: Cambridge, 1950.

Knight, Laura. *Oil Paint and Grease Paint.* Ivor Nicholson and Watson: London, 1936.

Lavery, Brian. *Churchill's Navy: The Ships, Men and Organisation, 1939–1945.* Conway: London, 2006.

Lewison, Jeremy (ed.) essay by Cork, Richard. *A Genius of Industrial England: Edward Wadsworth 1889–1949.* Arkwright Arts Trust and Bradford Galleries and Museums, Bradford. 1990.

McCabe, Lida Rose. 'Camouflage: War's Handmaid' in *Art World,* January 1918.

Marriott, Charles. 'Algernon Talmage (1871–1939)' in *Cornish Review,* spring, 1950.

Mottram, James Cecil. *Controlled Natural Selection and Value Marking.* Longmans, Green and Co.: London, 1914.

Muncaster, Martin. *The Wind in the Oak.* Robin Garton: London, 1978.

Murphy, Hugh and Bellamy, Martin. 'The Dazzling Zoologist – John Graham Kerr and the Early Development of Ship Camouflage' in *The Northern Mariner,* XIX, No.2, April 2009.

National Archives, Kew, London. See the Dazzle Painting records in ADM 1/8533/215; ADM 245/1-4; MT 25/16 and MT 25/67; and CAB 24/28/56. For the Naval Camouflage in Leamington Spa records see: ADM 212/122.

Newark, Tim. *Camouflage.* Thames and Hudson: London, 2007.

Newbolt, Henry. *Tales of the Great War.* Longmans, Green and Co.: London, 1916.

Newbolt, Henry. *Submarine and Anti-Submarine.* Longmans, Green and Co.: London, 1918.

Payne, Charles "Snaffles" Johnson. *Snaffles: A Half Century of Memories.* Collins: London, 1949.

Riding, Christine. (ed.) *Art and the War at Sea 1914–45.* Lund Humphries in association with the National Maritime Museum: London, 2015.

Roskam, A. *Dazzle Painting: Kunst Als Camouflage: Camouflage Als Kunst.* Exhibition catalogue. Stichting Kunstprojecten en Uitgeverij Van Spijk: Rotterdam, 1987.

The Royal Academy of Arts exhibition catalogue of 'Works by Camoufleur Artists', winter, 1919. (See: http://www.racollection.org.uk/ixbin/indexplus?record=VOL6182)

Royal Commission on Awards to Inventors. National Archives, Kew. (For records of Norman Wilkinson's claim: T173/522 and for Professor John Grahm Kerr's claim: TS 32 /19B.)

Smith, R. D. A. *Jan and Cora Gordon: Life, art, travel & music.* http://janandcoragordonart.blogspot.co.uk/ and http://www.pbase.com/hajar/art_of_jan_and_cora_gordon

Stein, Gertrude. *Picasso.* (Originally published in 1938.) Dover Publications: New York/London, 1984.

Stokes, Alan Gardner Folliott. 'Algernon Talmage (1871–1939)' in *The Studio* magazine. Vol.48, 1910.

Taylor, James. *Your Country Needs You: The Secret History of the Propaganda Poster.* Saraband: Glasgow, 2013.

Thayer, Gerald Handerson. *Concealing Coloration in the Animal Kingdom.* MacMillan: New York, 1909; 2nd ed., 1918.

Warner, Everett L. 'The Science of Marine Camouflage Design' in *Transactions of the Illuminating Engineering Society,* No.5, July 21, 1919.

Warner, Everett L. 'Fooling the Iron Fish: The Inside Story of Marine Camouflage' in *Everybody's Magazine,* November 1919.

White, Nelson C. *Abbott H. Thayer: Painter and Naturalist.* Connecticut Printers, Hartford, Connecticut, 1951.

Whittaker, Ben. *Zig-Zag Dazzle Ships.* Published online as part of the Liverpool Biennial Festival of Contemporary Art, 2016. See: http://www.biennial.com/journal/issue-4/zigzag-dazzle-ships

Wickham, Annette. 'Designed to Dazzle'. Online article on the 'role of the Royal Academy of Arts in the creation of dazzle camouflage during the First World War 1'. http://www.biennial.com/journal/issue-4/designed-to-dazzle

Williams, David. *Liners in Battledress: Wartime Camouflage and Color Schemes for Passenger Ships.* Conway: London, 1989.

Williams, David. *Naval Camouflage, 1914–1945: A complete visual reference.* US Naval Institute Press, Annapolis, 2001.

Wilkinson, Norman. *The Dardanelles – Colour Sketches from Gallipoli.* Longmans, Green and Co.: London, 1915.

Willis, Sam. 'How did an artist help Britain fight the war at sea?' http://www.bbc.co.uk/guides/zty8tfr

Wilkinson, Norman and Kerr, John Graham. Papers on 'The Dazzle Painting of Ships' (1919), published on behalf of the North-East Coast Institution of Engineers and Shipbuilders, which presented them at their Victory Meeting in Newcastle-upon-Tyne on 10 July 1919.

Wilkinson, Norman. 'The Dazzle Painting of Ships' in *RSA Journal,* 12 March 1920.

Wilkinson, Norman. 'Naval Camouflage' in *Encyclopaedia Britannica.* Vol.xxix, 11th edition/12th edition combined, 1922.

Wilkinson, Norman. *A Brush with Life.* Seely Service and Company: London, 1969.

Wilkinson, Norman. 'The Dazzle Painting of Ships,' (1919) as reprinted (in abridged form) in Bustard, James. *Camouflage.* Exhibition catalogue, Edinburgh: Scottish Arts Council, 1988.

Witt, David L. *Modernists in Taos: From Dasburg to Martin.* Red Crane Books: Santa Fe, 2002

Yardley, Edward *Frank Henry Mason: Marine Painter and Poster Artist,* Colley Books: Derbyshire, 2015.

INDEX